DEAR CATHY ... LOVE, MARY

DEAR CATHY . . .
LOVE, MARY

The year we grew up – tender, funny and
revealing letters from 1980s Ireland

Catherine Conlon and Mary Phelan

PENGUIN
IRELAND

PENGUIN IRELAND

UK | USA | Canada | Ireland | Australia
India | New Zealand |South Africa

Penguin Ireland is part of the Penguin Random House group of companies
whose addresses can be found at global.penguinrandomhouse.com.

Penguin
Random House
UK

First published 2015
001

Copyright © Catherine Conlon and Mary Phelan, 2015

The moral right of the authors has been asserted

Typeset by Palimpsest Book Production Limited, Falkirk, Stirlingshire
Printed in Great Britain by Clays Ltd, St Ives plc

A CIP catalogue record for this book is available from the British Library

ISBN : 978–1–844–88368–4

BAINTE DEN STOC

WITHDRAWN FROM DÚN LAOGHAIRE RATHDOWN
COUNTY LIBRARY STOCK

www.greenpenguin.co.uk

MIX
Paper from
responsible sources
FSC
www.fsc.org   FSC® C018179

Penguin Random House is committed to a
sustainable future for our business, our readers
and our planet. This book is made from Forest
Stewardship Council® certified paper.

To the memory of
Mary's parents, Peggy and Mickey
and
Catherine's father, Jack, and grandparents,
Kattie and Neddie

They gave us wings and encouraged us to fly . . .
. . . thirty years later our wings are only a little singed.

Contents

Prologue

My friendship with Catherine goes back to 1974. It was a special year for me. On the August bank-holiday weekend my family moved to a new house in Carrick-Beg, a terraced council house with running water. Our old home, further down the road in Carrick-Beg, was being knocked down by the council to make way for a scheme of sheltered housing for the elderly. Carrick-Beg is on the southern banks of the River Suir in Carrick-on-Suir, south Tipperary.

For me, the happiest aspect of the move was that it meant I had girls my own age living on either side – Anne-Marie to my right and Cheryl to my left. The following month, I returned to school. It was an exciting time as our school, the Presentation National School, had just merged with the Mercy National School so there were a whole lot of new faces to get used to.

Catherine Conlon's was one of those faces. She sat beside me that first day of third class and we hit it off straight away. She had glossy brown hair, which she sometimes wore in pigtails, and dark brown eyes. She was nine and five-twelfths while I was eight and eleven-twelfths (fractions were important that year). She was an inch taller than me. She spoke with a slight English accent, having been brought back to Ireland to live with her paternal grandparents, Kattie and Neddie, a few years earlier after her parents' divorce in London. Catherine idolised her dad, Jack, who stayed on in London, coming home each summer on holidays. She had no further childhood contact with her mother.

It may sound strange, but Catherine having divorced parents didn't seem like a big deal. Maybe it was because when I met her she was already living with her grandparents so I didn't know any different. And maybe it was because a lot of us had relations in the UK (where they had emigrated for work) and inevitably some of their marriages broke down and they got divorces there.

Catherine, on the other hand, recalls being acutely aware of being different. 'It was very difficult growing up in 1970s rural Ireland in a broken family. I thought "normal" people had a mam and a dad taking care of them, not grandparents. It was embarrassing and shameful to be children of absent parents. Looking back as an adult, I now see there were others in similar situations, but at the time I felt we really stuck out. Mary's home and family were a refuge for me. I not only had her friendship but also the love and support of her parents.'

Having had to grow up fast as the eldest of four girls, Catherine came across as much older than her years. Celia, her sister, was in the class behind us, and the twins, Lolo and Tish, were one year younger still. As a result, Catherine was a bossy big-sister type.

I had yearned for a big-sister type, bossy or otherwise. My brother, Martin (Matty), was seven years older than me. We were the much-wanted 'pigeon's clutch' of Peggy and Mickey. Before Martin, they had lost five babies (including twin boys), each born prematurely. My sister, Winifred, had lived only six weeks. I knew I had angels in Heaven looking out for me but what I wanted most was a real live sister to play and share with. Then along came Catherine.

Catherine introduced me to reading real books (i.e. those

without pictures) and we borrowed all the Secret Seven and Famous Five books that were in Carrick library. Together we figured out how to sort out life's great questions. In third class we had a wonderful teacher called Sister Antoinette. She was much younger than the other nuns and had new, interesting ways of teaching. Nonetheless, she also drilled us in spellings and maths tables. We had a spelling test every single day, one of those where you had to write down the spellings of ten words called out by the teacher, then hand over your copy to your neighbour to correct as the teacher called out the answers. Ten out of ten got a gold star. Catherine and I loved those gold stars. One day when we had both got one spelling wrong, we gave each other ten out of ten so we could each get a gold star. That night, neither of us could sleep with the guilt, thinking we were on the road straight to Hell for having lied and obtained a gold star by deception. Nothing would save us from eternal damnation except to own up. So first thing the following morning, we made our way up to Sister Antoinette with trembling knees to own up to our wrongdoing . . . only for her to allow us to keep the gold stars for being such 'good, honest girls' (while struggling to keep a straight face).

As we got older, we moved to Scoil Mhuire secondary school (Greenhill). We were thrilled to find we were in the same class and continued to sit beside each other. Catherine used to call to my house on Saturdays where I introduced her to music, playing whatever cassettes we had taped from the radio. We drank coffee and ate Peggy's apple tart. Peggy bought a coffee-table especially for us to use, and for years it was known in our house as 'Catherine's table'.

We were always chatting. When we weren't sitting chatting in our front room, we were sitting chatting in the Central Grill or Babby McCann's ice-cream parlour. And whenever we couldn't chat we would write to each other, especially during the long summer holidays from school. Very few houses had phones back then.

In 1983 Catherine and I sat the Leaving Cert. I was the first of my family to finish secondary school. It was the height of the recession and jobs were like hen's teeth. Most of Ireland had been hit badly but south Tipperary particularly so. Every year our French teacher in Greenhill arranged au-pairing jobs in a small town in Brittany called Trégunc, with which Carrick was twinned, and Catherine decided to go to France. By the end of that summer I had decided, after much angst, to become articled to a local firm of accountants in Tipperary while attending the Regional Technical College in Waterford.

Catherine and I promised faithfully to write to each other and we did pretty much every two weeks for a year. I well remember the thrill when I'd see the French stamp, the thick envelope and Catherine's familiar handwriting. And you could always tell the important bits – her writing would get messier because she'd been scribbling so fast to get all her thoughts down on the page. I kept Catherine's letters tied in a ribbon and in 1991 they were joined by my own when Catherine, home for her father's funeral, handed them back to me with the parting words, 'Sure, you might get these published some day.' We laughed at the idea that our girlish ramblings would ever mean anything to anyone. There they sat in my family home until last year. Peggy passed away in February, and in going through her things I came across the bundle of letters, still tied up with a big red ribbon.

In compiling them to be published we have either changed

some names, or used fake initials – Jane Austen style – and left out some of the really gossipy or private stuff that could land us in the courts. The letters that follow are most of what we wrote that year, and all of what we felt.

Mary Phelan
Dublin
Summer 2015

Part 1

Change

Autumn 1983

c/o Mme LeClercq
Le Restaurant
St Philibert
Trégunc
France

Friday, 26 August 1983

Dear Mary,

And before I say another word, let me warn you that this letter is most likely to be written at different intervals over the next few days, and consequently will be rather disjointed and somewhat peculiar.

At the moment I'm one of the few left sitting on the decks, watching the sun going down. Unfortunately it's rather cloudy so things are not as spectacular as one might hope. Nevertheless, the golden streaks of the sea, foam which is the most amazing shade of green (well, I suppose it is the water that is that colour), noise of the engines, smell of the chips and babble of French-accented voices all makes a rather pleasant calming scene.

Unbelievably, I'm not feeling sick and at one stage only felt rather dizzy. I can hardly believe it myself! I didn't even feel sick coming down to Cork from Tipperary in the car this morning.

I suppose I should give a quick rundown of the day. Left home after ten. Mrs B was giving a French girl a lift to Cork. She too is going to Roscoff. Her name's Valerie and she had been staying with Margaret Cooney as part of the town twinning. I thought I'd have a companion for the journey over. But she has a berth and I have a reclining chair.

Therefore, once we got aboard at about 2 p.m. we split up. I think it's just as well anyway. It would be too difficult and embarrassing to make conversation and besides I'd rather be independent, and not feel guilty every time I feel like taking a stroll or something.

Surprisingly enough, it took very little time to explore the boat. (Mrs B insists that a ship is bigger than this one! Maybe we should compromise and call it a ferry?) There are three decks all linked by stairs. The view of Ringaskiddy as we were pulling out was absolutely marvellous. Piles of colourful houses on a steep slope with a lovely church right in the centre. The boat is blue and white, smaller than I expected and surprisingly clean.

This afternoon it was really warm and I sat on a step reading. All of the chairs had been swiped before I came outside. Now, as most people have gone in for dinner, chairs are once more available. Mind you, they're not much more comfortable than the steps, which are made of steel.

I'm glad Mrs B was picking me up. But for more reasons than one. There was no time for last-minute goodbyes and emotional scenes this morning. But on reflection I cannot imagine any of my family getting all soppy and weepy. I suppose I'm being a bit premature but I don't feel homesick yet.

I was talking to Lena for about five minutes, who worked as au-pair for the family last year. She says the middle child, Delphine, is a bit of a handful. You wouldn't think it with that name, would you?

Oh, by the way, I rang Mrs Denny* to say goodbye to her on

---

* Our former English teacher.

Friday evening. I was talking to her for quite a while on the phone. I told her what Reggie* said about repeating the Leaving. But Denny said is there any point when I'm not really dying to take up a specific career – or words to that effect. Anyway, I think that by the time I got home on Thursday evening I'd decided not to repeat. I wish I could make up my mind and stick to one particular thing, but I seem incapable of doing so. I suppose you'd say it's a case of welcome-to-the-club!

Monday, 29 August, 10 p.m.

Hi again! Right now I'm curled up on a couch trying to balance a bowl of coffee, write this letter and understand a film on the TV. I suppose I should finish off where this letter began. On the ship I wandered around, ate, drank coffee, knitted and read until about twelve. Then, after much effort, I slept on my reclining chair to finally awaken at 4 a.m. Then I got up and wandered around, stepping over the sleeping bags of scruffy, bearded, greasy-headed French students (only the beards defining male from female!), hoping in vain to see the sun rise over the sea. But here the sun gets up after seven o'clock, and so I was out of luck!

Do us a favour, will you? Go up to Clonmel and punch the girl in the travel agency on the nose pour moi, because we docked in Roscoff at 6 a.m.! Got through Customs (could have had a case full of drugs and no problem) and waited 'til 7.15 a.m. when M. & Mme LeClercq arrived with son,

* Sister Regina, our former religion teacher.

daughter and nephew. Got into car, drove to St Philibert, a small village six km from Trégunc, and arrived at 9 a.m. Had brekky, went to visit Mme LeC's mother, returned to restaurant, leaving kids at Grandma's, had lunch, slept a little, read a little, wrote a little. Visited Grandma's again in Trégunc at about 4 p.m. Talk about being thrown in at the deep end!

For the first time in years, she had her four kids and their families gathered around. That left me struck dumb – well, slight exaggeration, I could say 'oui', 'non' and 'merci' (mercy!). In the crowd, ten adults and an army of kids. I wasn't ignored, far from it, but I was so tired and felt really shy and awkward not knowing what to do. Then the kids were all grumpy at each other and decided to demolish a tent. Only by chewing very hard on my lip could I prevent myself from bursting into tears. If there had been a ship home on Sunday night I'd be delivering this letter by hand! And I'm not joking. Well, the silver lining in yesterday's cloud is my first glass of champagne and that lining was only silver-plated. Perhaps one has to develop a taste for these things. Today, after a good night's sleep, I feel much better and perhaps I won't jump out of my dormer window after all.

I suppose I should describe the family. M. and Mme are both very nice, early thirties, I'd say, both dark-haired. She's very brown, but he looks positively anaemic. If I glued some of his skin onto this page, you wouldn't notice it! The oldest girl (twelve years) Chrystelle, after three meetings, strikes me as being very nice. But I have nothing to do with her. Delphine I've been warned about, as previously said. She's staying at her grandmother's now, so I cannot say more about her. Thomas should count himself lucky not to be floating

restaurant, having had
lunch, slept a little, rea
te a little. Visited Grand
Tregune at about 4.00
ut being thrown in at the d
Koo the first time in ge
her four kids & their
tered around. That left me
mb, well slight exaggerat
y "oui", "non" and "merci"
the crowd, ~~ten~~ adults & a
ds. I wasn't ignored, far
t I was so tired & feel
awkward not knowing what
e kids were all grumpy a
decided to demolish a ter
hewing ~~very~~ hard on my lip
~~venu~~ myself from tears
f ~~there~~ had been
or ~~Satud~~ Sunday
be delivering this
hand! & I'm not
de silver lining
cloud is my f
of champagne

face downward in the bath (pronounce the name as 'Tomah'). He's about two and I'd imagine is a very nice kid when he's not over-tired or sulking, which he has been for the past two days. He's a peculiar kid, really. Perhaps he's just shy at the moment. Lena liked him anyway, and I suppose I will too, when I'm leaving.

I love their house. I'd say at one stage it was a two-storeyed one, the second storey being extremely high. The first floor is the restaurant. It's quite large and furnished with wooden tables and red-white checked tablecloths and lamps and curtains. Nine people work there. I don't know if that includes Mme and M. But I've met some of the staff as we have lunch and supper together, before the place opens to the public.

There are two girls – both fairly nice. Then there are three boys; one blond, quite attractive, one dark, <u>very</u> attractive, and one curly-haired, dark and sitting beside me, so that's the end of that description! (The other two sit across from me.) The third boy is getting some teasing because he is eating very little. I don't know if it's because he is on a diet or waiting for the results of the Bac. They're all pleasant enough, I'd imagine, even though I'm incapable of speaking to them!

To return to my original description of the house – well, I'd say the second storey was divided in two. Downstairs is the huge kitchen/sitting-room. In a corner is an adorable spiral staircase leading upwards (where else?). About half of the second floor then is covered by our bedroom and the bathroom and toilet which we use – there being another one downstairs for the parents.

I share a room with Chrystelle (I love the spelling of it) and Delphine but have it to myself at the moment as they are both away. They have bunk beds. I think they have the same type on *Diff'rent Strokes*. My bed is just under the sloping roof, beside the window.

Well, that's enough of descriptions except to say the Catholic church is across the road and yesterday I went to Mass there, even though I couldn't understand a word of it. It was the feast day of St Philibert and afterwards there was a procession led by women wearing the traditional Breton costumes, which you are doubtless familiar with, Mary!

Also right outside the restaurant is a bloody funfair and the guy in charge of records has a passion for Rod Stewart and played 'Baby Jane' four times in a row as I was trying to sleep last night! They play music the whole time, much of it in English. Hark? There's David Bowie and 'Let's Dance'. But I'll be glad when the carnival goes tomorrow let me tell you.

I never thought I'd say it, but, boy, do I regret all of those hours I slept during Nolan's French class! I can barely open my mouth. I wish I'd slept more often during Irish class, though, because every time I wish to indicate that I don't understand (which is very often) I feel a burning desire to say 'Gabh mo leithscéal'! I have a lot of French in my head but it's just trying to say it that's so hard. It would be much easier to write it. Even now, here and there, I feel the need to write a word in French. I suppose by this time next week I'll be able to talk a bit more. I hope so. Oh, there's Kajagoogoo with 'Too Shy'. That's me! Telly is hopeless tonight, so I keep turning it up and down with the remote control. Down when I hear a good song from the carnival outside and up when Rod Stewart comes on, which is often, about every third song!

I don't think I need to have any worries about competing

with Lena. When I first arrived Mme asked me if I smoked. Then her relations asked me the same thing. I finally plucked up enough French and courage to ask why everyone wanted to know and breathed a sigh of relief when I said, 'No.' Mme said that Lena was a chain smoker and there were cigarettes everywhere, even in the children's beds (I got suspicious there – my evil mind, I suppose!). She elaborated then about Lena. She went out nearly every night, to return at three or four and then rose at about twelve. Also, she never played with Thomas, etc. My spirits lifted a bit there. But I sympathise with Lena as far as Thomas is concerned as I cannot imagine him playing with anybody!

Did I mention food before? Well, it's lovely, particularly the bread, which is delicious. (I should have written that in capital letters, I think.) It's quite simple food, nothing outlandish really, so far anyway. Although this evening for supper there were prawns or something (about five inches long with claws, etc. D'you know what they are?). Not knowing what way to eat them anyway, I said I didn't like them (how sophisticated!) and was met with amazed stares from everybody. But I made up for it with the pizza, which was delicious. Also, there were boiled eggs, halved and served with a sauce, and cauliflower. But I doubt if you'd like it, even though I loved it! By the way, everybody just pulled the fish apart with their hands à la Henry VIII!

Well, that's my sadistic act over for tonight. I suppose your mother will have to go and buy you a new pair of eyes tomorrow after trying to decipher this lengthy scribble. I'd be grateful (eternally!) if you could pass this on to Sue if you happen to see her. I'll probably write to her later (oh, God,

Rod Stewart again!). As a matter of fact, I'll certainly write to her. However, I've no intention of going into long descriptions again, having already had to do it for the Clan in Glen* (great title for a book, eh?) and tomorrow I'll have to do it for Daddy, I expect. I suppose really I should invest in a photocopying machine.

If you meet the Clan from Glen don't mention that only the fact that Brittany Ferries sails once a week to Cork, and I can only do thirty strokes doggy paddle, prevented me from returning home on Monday morning. In my letter to them I emphasised the champagne bit. Otherwise Grandma wouldn't sleep a wink until I'd arrive home and that certainly wouldn't do, would it?

Mary, please, please, please write soon and tell me <u>all</u> the news, all the little unimportant bits and pieces (gossip!) because I suppose by this time next week I'll be very homesick.

Missing you all already,
Tons of love
Catherine

PS Be sure and say hello to all of the family for me and tell your mother to hang onto the coffee-table until you get my next letter at least.

PPS Hi, Sue, if you read this. Please say hello to your family too and everyone else that you know that knows me.

---

* Catherine's grandparents and younger sisters.

Carrick

Wednesday, 7 September 1983

Dear Cathy,

I was thrilled to bits to get your letter (on Monday). It was actual proof that you were really in Trégunc. All week I kept expecting you to turn up on my doorstep saying that the boat had sunk or gone on fire or . . . or . . . Anyway, Kitty there was I still in bed and I heard the pitter-patter of a letter (it rhymes!) on the floor. Me Mammy got all excited and of course I had to get up and read it to her. You should have seen her face: talk about winning the Sweeps.

Anyway, I was delighted everything went okay on the crossing. Tell me one thing. How did you recognise M. et Mme LeClercq? I have pictures of you going around Roscoff tugging at coat sleeves pleading 'Gabh mo leathscéal, could you tell me if est-ce que vous êtes les LeClercqs?'!

What are the parents' first names? By the way, I saw Lena this day last week. I was coming down the steps (onto the New Bridge) when I could see her in the distance (as they say in the ad 'she shines out at you'). She looked gorgeous with a white billowing dress.

Well, anyway, here I am sitting in my room at 12.40 p.m. It's very dull outside, kinda misty, and just the day for stayin' in bed (which I did up to half an hour ago). Today is the Abortion Referendum day. Every now and then a car goes past and a loudspeaker hollers, 'VOTE YES, VOTE YES, VOTE YES' (maybe it's stuck). Talking about that, who should come along yesterday as Mam was gardening (well, that's what she calls it)? Only a friend – or sort of friend – of Martin's. She was campaigning for abortion!

Dear Cathy,
          I was thrilled
get your letter (on Monday,
proof that you were real
week I kept expecting you
on my doorstep saying
had sank or gone on fi
Anyway, Kitty there was
and I heard the pitte
letter (it rhymns!) on the
Mommy got all excited
I had to get up and
You should have seen he
about winning the Swe
          Anyway I was

I needn't tell you Martin got some teasing when he came home from work.

Oh, by the way, remember me telling you I went for the interview with Walsh & Gilligan, the accountants? They were supposed to give me an answer the following Monday or Tuesday. Monday came – no sign of no one (oh, the grammar!). Tuesday came. At around six o'clock I was giving up when who should come along? Only Mr Walsh. He said they were taking me on (sounds like a boxing challenge, uh?) and he wanted to know if I'd sent away the application to the Regional and for the grant. I was still waiting for the application form for the Regional but I had the grant form. He helped me to fill it in. It had to be in by 5 p.m. the next day. It was too late to post it at that stage so guess what? Martin cycled all the way to Clonmel on Wednesday and handed it in! Thirteen miles each way! (Meanwhile I posted the Regional application.) Anyway, they asked Martin for proof of Da's earnings (pension books, etc.). I had no way of getting them up on Thursday. Mammy even stopped (hijacked) people on the street but absolutely no one was going to Clonmel ('cos it was Piltown Show Day and they were all going in the opposite direction!). I then had to race from phone box to phone box looking for the VEC phone number – none of them had an intact phone book! I phoned Sue. Her mother answered and gave me the shock of my life. 'Sue's in HOSPITAL,' says she. 'Wha'?' says I. Whereupon she proceeded to tell me that Sue was gone in for her eye operation. Phew! Anyway, I phoned again on Monday and Sue herself answered it. She said she felt fine but her eye was sore enough. They tightened the muscle (aaargh!). Just as we were having a good chat someone came along for the phone so I had to ring off with the promise that I'd phone again.

Now, before I proceed any further I must fill you in on what happened that Thursday night. Who should come along on his bike at around half past eight? Only Sue's brother, Gerard. Mam and I were sitting on the garden seat, whereupon this fella stopped in the middle of the road and stared in. It took me a few seconds to recognise him. I went out to him and we spent ages chatting. People were going out on the town – we were chatting. It turned dark – we were chatting. The stars came out (well, to tell the truth there weren't many) – we were chatting. People came home from being out on the town – we were still chatting. After chatting about everything under the sun (including YOU), he finally left at around quarter to eleven or so. He sure is easy to talk to, isn't he? But the funniest thing that happened was, while we were talking, who should pass down? Only some girls from school. When they got to the Kickham's [pub] they rushed over to Martin, asking who was the gorgeous-looking fella I was seen talking to? (I actually think I climbed up a peg in their esteem!) I've been getting strange looks ever since.

Hang on, I've got to go eat my din-dins. Be back soon . . .

How ya? It's me again. Anyway, to get back to the VEC grant, I finally got a lift up to Clonmel on Friday from Mickey Norris (a neighbour) after me da had twisted his arm. Of course, I missed them when I came out of the Tech and so I decided to do a little exploring around the shops. Well, after all, it's not every day a culchie like meself gets to explore the metropolis! I went into Mirror Mirror. They've got some gorgeous drop-waisted skirts but they've also got a lot of junk. You can imagine the cursing when I finally came back to the car – an hour later!

So here I am at the moment waiting for the Regional reply. I don't feel absolutely 100 per cent sure about accountancy as a career but God knows I've got to start somewhere. Oh, by the way (here comes my mother enquiring what the smell is – I sprayed some Impulse to mask the pong of pig slurry wafting in the window from the pig farm up the hill), Sue passed some remark about you being able to go to college when you come back. You know, if she mentions college again, I'll wilfully throttle her.

I went over town on Monday just as everyone was coming home from school. It felt really funny not to be part of it all. They made me feel about ninety-nine. I saw Miss Nolan. I called into Galvins [bakery]. Anne has finished up her summer job there. I also met Margaret L. Did you know that she was repeating? I stopped to talk to her. She looked really down. You know she got the place in the art college (which is nigh on impossible to get into) but she can't get the grant 'cos she failed Maths. It's really tough luck. She got a B in Honours English and all.

Now for the GOSSIP. Ahm. Well. Um. E— has stopped drooling over V— (praise Allah!). I met Wendy on Monday night. She was going to the pictures (*Superman* – groan!). She's not doing anything at the moment and she was in a hurry and didn't say much.

The telly has been good the past few days. Last Monday night week, the James Last concert was on from Tralee. It was ABSOLUTELY FAB. There was a great range of music played – classical, slow and romantic, rock and roll, Irish ballads – even jigs and reels (whereupon the crowd broke into the 1, 2, 3, 4, 5, 6, 7). I really enjoyed it and would have loved to have been in Tralee. While watching I was eating a burger from the Grill. I bit in too hard, knocked out my filling and broke a bit off my tooth.

All last week it was cutting the tongue off me and I wath going around the plathe with a thlight lithp. It's worn down now, though.

We also saw the Rose of Tralee on Tuesday and Wednesday. Miss Carrick won. Her name's Brenda Hyland, and she was representing Waterford at the Finale. On Sunday, we had the All-Ireland. I really enjoyed the match (or should I say matches – the one between Cork and Kilkenny and the one between Ma and Da?). Ma was for Kilkenny. Every time they scored she'd go dancing around and Da would use profane language and vice versa for Cork. Da kept accusing her of being disloyal to her province of Munster whereupon Ma tried to persuade him that Kilkenny <u>was</u> in Munster (honestly!).

You should have seen us trying to photograph the pussies the other day. Dandy (doggy Walsh) came peeping around. The camera was aimed at him whereupon he cocked his leg! Mammy gave such a roar of laughter that the dog ran for cover! I haven't seen him since. Listen, I'd better shurrup 'cos I'm running out of paper, inspiration, gossip and immaculate writing. If you don't write soon I'll kill you. Write back giving me a blow by blow account of your <u>working</u> (tee-hee) day.

Lots of love,
byeeeeeeee,
from Mary (as if you didn't know)

PS Oops, I forgot, how's your French coming along?

PPS Everyone wishes you the best. Byeeeee.

PPPS I got a letter from my penpal in California. She's getting married in January!

PPPPS When Da saw tons of love written on the end of your letter he started laughing. I asked him what he was laughing for, and me ma wittily replied that he wasn't used to giving love in tons, only ounces!

Trégunc

Friday, 16 September 1983

Dear Mary,

Thanks a million for your really long letter. It took so long to arrive, I was beginning to examine my conscience and think over the last few days I'd spent in Ireland. Also, a huge big CONGRATULATIONS on your being accepted at W & G. You say you're not sure if you want to be an accountant, but at least it's better than going to the Tech for a secretarial course.

Also, before I go a step further, I would absolutely love to kill you! You say you were talking to Gerard about me, but you never said <u>what</u> you said. A word-for-word account, if you please! I can just imagine all the neighbours peeking out the window at the two of you! Were you inside the gate or outside? And, yes, he is very easy to talk to. Remember I told you about the night he came over to Glen to collect Sue's bike? I could tell the two twins were absolutely dumbfounded. And only for it was so dark he probably would have stayed longer. I'll bet your parents gave you some teasing! Had they met him before?

Did you know Celia has gone back to London? She's got her own tiny flat and is going to work full-time for Pops. I think she's also going to night classes. I think she made the right choice.

I suppose I'd better tell you a bit of news from this neck of the woods, not that there are many woods around. It's been so long since I wrote to you that I cannot really remember what I said. But as it was only the day after I arrived I couldn't have told you much.

For the first week or so I was really miserable. I'd liked everything except the youngest child Thomas, aged 2½. He spent hours upon hours of every day and night just screaming his head off. I thought he didn't like me. I was seriously thinking of taking the boat home. I remember the first Wednesday Daddy phoned at lunch time. I chatted to him for five minutes or so. When I hung up, I got all weepy and sad again. I went back to my place, and tried to act as normal as possible, stuffing forkfuls of food into my mouth, which I couldn't swallow because my throat was all blocked up. Boy, did I feel stupid sitting there with tears streaming down my face. And I'm not exaggerating. Well, at least everybody had the sense to totally ignore me and carry on chatting amongst themselves!

But now I'm really settled in. I even phoned Daddy one night and was talking to him for twenty minutes (cost IR£5!) and when I hung up I didn't feel in the least bit down in the dumps! He's talking of coming over here for a few days sometime. I hope he does.

Oh, yes! I suppose I should say I've been asked (indirectly) to stay on and I think I probably will, at least until Christmas. But to tell the truth, I really don't know why they want me as I have so little to do. I just sort of keep an eye on the kids and keep Thomas's milk bottle full. I give him a bath at night, put him in his pyjamas and go for a walk. He generally goes to bed at ten or eleven, which is an absolute scandal for a young kid. But the first week when I arrived I used to put him to bed at around eight and he screamed and screamed, and Chrystelle or François used to come and take him up again. So now I just leave him to do as he pleases!

Since he started school (yes, school!) he has really improved, though. D'you remember hearing about the école maternelle? Well, that's where he's going from 9 a.m. until 4.30 p.m. and I go with him and stay there all day. It's really ironic, isn't it? There I was finished with school for good and now I'm back on the bottom rung!

I don't really know why Vivianne wants me to go with him. The teacher is terribly nice and is quite capable of looking after him, but then, who am I to disagree? The kids just play at school. You know, things like putting shapes into their proper holes and that sort of thing. Despite the fact that Thomas is young, he's quite capable of fending for himself and doesn't really need me at all. So I have very little to do. I write letters, knit and read.

You may remember Mrs B saying that the second girl, Delphine, was a bit of a minx; well, I've absolutely no problems with her. Of course, like all kids, she misbehaves now and again, e.g. turning on the light to read at six o'clock in the morning (I share a room with the two girls), but I just yell at her and she usually gets the message. Chrystelle is very nice but she really spoils Thomas. François and Vivianne are quite strict with them and they are well brought-up and well-mannered as a rule.

The whole family seems to like me and are anxious for me to stay on. Chrystelle has started English as she just went to secondary school this year. Vivianne will go to night classes to learn it soon and so they want me to help them with it, which I'm quite looking forward to doing.

I suppose you can remember how awful I was at oral French in Nolan's class. It's so much harder to speak it than to write it. For the first week or so here, I hardly opened my mouth. I'm improving a little bit now, though. It's absolutely amazing how much French I'd forgotten over the summer holidays. But my vocab, which never was very wide, is steadily improving. I think my accent is a little better too.

At the moment the restaurant they run is open from 12 to 2 p.m. and 7.30 to 9 p.m. But of course by the time they finish up completely it's usually 3 p.m. and up to about midnight. After next week, though, due to lack of customers, they won't open at all at night. So, in the evenings the whole family will be together. I'm looking forward to that as they are all really nice. Vivianne, who is terrific at handcrafts, has promised to teach me how to crochet, make lace, do tapestries, etc. They bought a video recorder last week and also have piles of records, although I haven't seen them yet. So winter should be quite cosy, I hope!

I suppose I should fill you in on the restaurant staff. At the moment there are three, but I think in peak season there are five or six, besides Vivianne and François that is.

Chantal is in her early twenties and is the waitress. She's very nice, quite friendly, has blonde hair and isn't what one thinks French girls look like. In other words Brigitte Bardot has no competition from her.

Bruno also has blond hair, is about twenty-two, and is quite tall and reasonably good-looking. He can speak a little English. But he is one of the funniest people I've ever met. He's a great mimic and can say the funniest things in the most serious way! He's the sort of person you hate eating with because you keep choking on your food. He loves to show off his English by talking to me in it in front of the others, none of whom can speak it. He's the waiter.

Then we come to Yvan, who is absolutely, totally and utterly gorgeous! He's got dark hair, very dark eyes and beautiful bone structure. You mightn't believe this, but I don't know what his teeth are like! At mealtimes he sits across from me at the table and often I catch him staring at me, which is a great morale booster, but nothing more. He too is very funny. I think he helps François with the cooking. He's twenty-four or twenty-five. But one day at dinner Thomas was misbehaving and refused to sit down and Viv said to Yvan, 'Does your son act like this at the table?' in French, of course. I'm sure that's what she said to him. And I thought, Shucks! But on Wednesday the new video recorder arrived and after work Chantal and Yvan came up to watch a film. They were sitting together on the couch holding hands! And I know for definite they're not married to each other. So now I don't know if he is or isn't married. Hey. I've thought of something – maybe he's an unmarried father!

Apart from these three, though, I haven't even seen any other young people around St Philibert. I think some kind of plague knocked off everyone between the ages of ten and thirty. As a result I'm very lonely and at the moment that's really the only cloud on the horizon.

Every evening after I've fixed up the kids I go out walking for about an hour. It gets dark around 9 p.m. Mostly I go along the coast road. There are lots of lovely little beaches and the scenery is really beautiful. I love looking at all the big rocks along by the road. Also there are quite a few teeny-weeny islands in the bay, which are nice to look at. When it gets fairly dark I can see two lighthouses. One is red and the other is yellow. They're lovely. In a little bay about two miles up the road there are about 100 little boats. They're absolutely beautiful especially in the evening because the sun goes down behind them. There's also a lovely pier with a lighthouse at the end – a real postcard scene!

But again I never ever see anybody. I know Lena had lots of friends but that was in peak season and she was able to meet them on the beach. Also there are absolutely hundreds of holiday homes around here and the owners live in places like Paris. Of course they're all gone home for the winter. Also I don't know if I'd like Lena's friends. I don't think they'd be quite my sort. Viv was saying that she used to go out to discos, etc., almost every night and often didn't get in until about 4 a.m. I was rather surprised to learn that. So you can see why I don't think I'd be nuts about Lena's pals here. But if I don't meet somebody of my own age soon, I declare to God, I'll go out of my mind!

Oh, I nearly forgot, the first few nights I was here, I left my bedroom window wide open. After two or three days, I noticed these lumps all over one side of my face and on my legs and hands. At first I thought I was allergic to the food or something. But then I found out that they were mosquito bites. I scratched the ones on my limbs and now am all scars. Luckily enough, the ones on my face weren't itchy and after a while they eventually faded leaving no signs.

I think I've more or less run out of news now. Except I had a letter from Daddy at the beginning of the week and he said that the twins <u>might</u> be going over to London for Christmas.

I'd already told him I hope to be there for Christmas. If we are all in London then, it'll be the first time the five of us (Daddy, Celia, Tish, Lolo and me) have been together in fourteen years for 25 December. But somehow or another I cannot see it getting off the ground.

Please write soon and let me know how you all are in Carrick. Also did my eyes deceive me or did a girl from Carrick (she's forty-ish, isn't she?) really win the Rose of Tralee? Please pass on any information you have about anybody and write soon. Best of luck in your new job.

Love,
Catherine

(I was going to write 'bons baisers de' but that brings back too many bad memories of French class!)

PS Be sure and tell your parents that I was asking for them.

PPS I don't believe E— has stopped boring the whole world with her passion for E—.

PPPS Weather here is very miserable at the moment. It rains a lot and there are a lot of 'tempests'.

PPPPS At Roscoff, I had the LeClercqs' name announced. When they arrived (a little late) they went to the reception desk and the girl pointed me out. But I recognised them from photos Lena had shown me. So we all sorta met halfway across the floor.

Carrick

Monday, 26 September 1983

Dear Catherine,

I'm writing this letter sitting on my bed upstairs. It's really sunny here today – just like summer. I was thrilled to bits to get your letter the other day. I was in bed when it came but it sure woke me up. I'm glad that you're settling in grand.

The last few days here have been hell for me. Last Friday I spent all afternoon trying to get through to the Regional on the phone. Me mam was with me and she nearly drove me bonkers. When I finally got thru – guess what? – yer man was gone home. I came home in a really bad mood, not being able to make up my mind whether I'd go for the Civil Service interview in Dublin next Thursday, whether I'd stick to the accountancy, or whether I'd jump in the Suir! Common sense prevailed and I phoned the Regional again today. I'm starting tomorrow for the accountancy (though the rest of them started last Monday). I then went to Walsh & Gilligan where I had to sign the contract and I've got to bring me da over around three o'clock this afternoon to witness it 'cos I'm underage. Now that I've signed it I think I've made the biggest mistake of my whole life but here goes – I'll be twenty-four before I'm out of it! The Regional should be an experience anyhow.

Anyway, I'll put that subject away now. Did you know we had the Macra na Feirme AGM, in the Bess [Bessborough Arms Hotel]? I was showing your letter to Sue when who should appear but P—, whereupon we made a fuss of hiding the letter, hoping to arouse suspicions. He started grinning (ooh!); we started blushing. Nothing's changed. The rest of the meeting was pretty routine. Oh, yeah, I nearly forgot. Tom (blue jeep and eyes) was elected chairman. Pat was elected treasurer. And there was I, 99 per cent certain that I wouldn't join again. But the thought of missing that soft voice every fortnight ... I'm not a masochist after all – so I'm undecided now (what's new?).

There's no gossip happening. It's absolutely dead around here. I should have done something like you. Actually I keep hearing that from Ma, with whom relations have been strained over the last few days. There was a full-scale row on Friday, but it's blown over now. Nothing like excitement, huh! Oh by the way, my maman says, 'Thank card for the Catherine'. I'm not joking – that's what she actually said! The card was lovely, though.

I suppose you've heard that Tina's gone back repeating as well as Cooney, Suzanne, Patricia and many more. Come to think of it, not many of us leavers got jobs. I think they are mad (nuts mad) to repeat. The competition for jobs will be worse next year. I was really over the moon that Eleanor got accepted for nursing. She cycled all the way in to tell me last Friday week. She really deserves it, don't you think? Meanwhile Sue is driving people nuts about college. I phoned Anne Maher and she swore she'd never phone Sue again as last time she got a lecture on why she should have gone to college. NEVER YOU MIND what Gerard and I said about you. All I can say is that he was very complimentative [sic] – and I was surprised at his observance [sic].

I'm delighted for Celia. I agree that she's made the right decision. Somebody told me the twins were thinking of leaving too. Is that true?

Oh, I must ask you: do you spend ALL day at school with Thomas? What about lunch? How far away is the school? (It's like *Mastermind*, huh?) Best of luck with the French guys – Bruno and Yvan. It won't be long before, as the ad says, they 'can't resist your womanly wiles, they'll be powerless to resist . . . shouldn't be allowed'!

If you would like me to send you on the *Carrick Opinion* or the *Munster Express* I'd be delighted. No trouble. Honest!

Listen, I'd better shurrup and bring my da over to W & G to sign the contract. I'll give you a blow-by-blow account of college in my next letter. (By the way, Alma Grace has been elected to Foróige in Faugheen. I saw it in the paper.) Sorry I haven't much news. The only thing that happened in Carrick lately is the death of a four-year-old boy. He had jaundice and meningitis and other complications. Everyone here sends you their best. Write soon 'cos it takes so long for the letters in the post anyway.

Cheryl is working in town, babysitting for her cousin's baby, Emma (three months). She's adorable (Emma, that is!). Cheryl comes over every second day and I also go over to her. We went to the pictures together last Wed night. We thought it might be good 'cos John Cleese was in it but it was USELESS. There were only eighteen or so other people there and they weren't even interested in the film (if you get my drift). Anyway, AU REVOIR (Da's going mad calling me so I'd better go).

God bless
Mary

PS Any chance of you popping a Jean-Claude or Pierre into an envelope as a pressie for me? PLEASE. XX

PPS I miss you lots.

Trégunc
(beach near St Phil)

Tuesday afternoon, 4 October 1983

Dear Mary,

Thanks a million for your letter, which arrived yesterday.
Congrats on finally committing yourself to something, even if
you'll spend the rest of your life kicking yourself (welcome to
the club!). The advice of Auntie Cathy is to remember if you
were sitting in a Civil Service office somewhere you'd
probably be doing the very same thing. So keep your chin up!

The fact that Catherine Cummins will be in your class in
WRTC should cheer you up. At least, I expect she's in your
class as I had a letter from her last week and she said she's
doing accountancy.

The same day I received a letter from Sue. I could've
bloody well killed her. Here I am, dying to hear some news,
and she sends me the results of the US Open Tennis, not to
mention Brands Hatch Grand Prix! If you can bear a lecture
on colleges ring her up some time and ask her about me and
Dublin Institute of Technology. It's not as mysterious as it
sounds!

I also got a letter from Eleanor. She gave me a run-down
on the Macra AGM (I knew I should've stayed at home and
joined!). I was laughing so much that Annique started giving
me funny looks. I read the letter at school, you see. I'd love if
you could send on the photograph of the whole crowd. Also
I'd be eternally grateful if you'd send on the 'Carrick Notes'
from the *Munster* or *Opinion*. There's no need to go to the

bother of sending on the whole paper. Thanks a million for thinking of offering.

Daddy rang me on Saturday night (oh, his phone bill). I was also talking to Celia and I got a letter from her today. She's settling in well in her flat. I believe she's starting secretarial college this week. As far as I can make out, she goes full-time for six weeks. Then she works in the office a few days and goes to college for a few days. Not bad, huh?

Daddy says he'll try and come over here for a few days. I hope he'll be able to manage it. But at the moment he's busy at work, as he has been for the past fourteen years! Just the same I'm keeping my fingers crossed!

And while I think of it, you horrible, mean, cruel, awful (oh, yuk! I've just seen a <u>lizard</u>!) creature, if you don't tell me what you and Gerard said about me I'll be forced to take further action, like writing to him! Using words like 'observant' and 'complimentary', indeed! Getting me all curious and nosy! D'you know the cliché 'with friends like that . . .' Please, please, give me some indication, clue, tidbit of what you said, please.

I haven't forgotten that tomorrow is your birthday. When I get up I'm going to sing 'Happy Birthday To You' I promise. I was afraid to buy you a pressie, though, as I'm sure it would either get lost or broken in the post. So I'm afraid you'll have to wait until I come home again.

To tell you the truth I don't know why you want a Jean-Claude or Pierre. Me, I'd make do with a Michael any day. And don't you <u>dare</u> tell R—. You know what a big mouth she has, and although I like it over here, I don't want to be exiled for life!

JEAN-CLAUDE

JEAN

CLAUDE

PIERRE

(By the way, I hope you're keeping all of these letters, so that they can be published when I'm rich and famous, or alternatively can be used by M. Sherlock Holmes as clues if I'm murdered or anything over here! End of diversion.)

You may notice that the quality of my writing has deteriorated somewhat. My God, says you, could it possibly get any worse? Well, it's due to the fact that a four-inch lizard and a heavy tide forced me to evacuate the tiny corner of the beach I was sitting in. So now I'm sitting overlooking the Atlantic, while a force seven wind keeps blowing my paper away. And if it succeeds, you'll understand why this letter makes even less sense than all of the others!

You were asking me about school. Well, firstly, it's about the same distance away as you are from St Mary's graveyard. And, yes, I do go there all day every day with Thomas, i.e. Monday, Tuesday, Thursday, Friday, half-day Saturday. The other days are free. So you can understand I get terribly bored at times. My main occupations are writing, reading and knitting. Some afternoons, though, while the younger kids, including Thomas, are asleep, I go for a walk or, if it's really warm, to the beach. Mind you, today it's freezing.

As I haven't enough wool at the moment to make something for myself, I've started knitting for the dolls at school. Yesterday I made a dress and cap for one of them. It turned out very well, even if I do say so myself. The doll was named after me!

I really must describe some of my <u>école maternelle</u> students to you. Yes, the word is 'my'. I'm teaching them English, believe it or not. Of course progress is slow, but then there's no rush. I love doing it, but I wish I was able to sing.

It'd make things a lot easier, especially as I'm trying to teach them 'One Little, Two Little, Three Little Indians . . .' at the moment. It's harder for them to pick up the tune with the way I croak!

Well, now, descriptions! Top of the list is the teacher's little girl. Her name is Anne. She's 2½, blonde hair, pale skin with freckles on her nose, small, plump, cuddly, gorgeous, and the kind of kid I'd like to have myself sometime. She's always happy, or nearly always; she's affectionate, clever, generous (she gives me a 'bite' of her bikkie every day!) and, as you've probably guessed, I'm nuts about her. So is everybody else. She spent about twenty minutes today chucking her teddy bear over the playground wall, while everybody fought for the honour of retrieving it and handing it back! She's like one of those girls you see in the toddlers-kissing-each-other posters. Of course, she's not perfect, but even when she thumps Thomas over the head he just laughs. If anybody else did that he'd scream for a week at least!

Then there's Marina, who's five or six – a lovely blonde-haired kid. As a matter of fact, the majority of the kids are blonde-haired. Marina's very clever, lazy and will be a leader some day.

Carole, blonde-haired, brown-eyed, will be a stunner; as will Karen, whose description is the same. They're very friendly, cheerful and well-behaved, gorgeous kids. I love them.

Then comes Marie, who's an absolute chatterbox and keeps giving me funny looks when I exclaim 'quel dommage', 'horrible', etc., in her few stops for breath. (There goes Anne chucking her poor bear over the wall again!) Aurélie,

Melanie, Audrey, Laetitia, Grizalia, Caroline are some of the other girls.

Next, the boys. There are two brothers here, Louis (three) and Vincent (six) either of whom could accompany Anne in her poster. Louis particularly is gorgeous. Huge big eyes and thick blond hair. The two of them have lovely characters and along with Anne are my favourites, though naturally I don't show any favouritism, I hope!

Nicolas (don't pronounce the *s*) has beautiful, almost white hair, blue eyes, perfect teeth, terrific smile, and is the greatest monster since King Kong! His hobby is fighting, kicking people, belting them over the head, and other such gentle pastimes.

Patrice is a pig! In plain simple language. I won't go into descriptions of any of the others, but I'll give you a few of their names. There's Erwan, Yvon, Ewann, William, Stefan, Philippe, Julien and another Nicolas, who's as bad as the first one!

I go back to the restaurant for lunch at 11.30 a.m. every day. The kids all eat here at school at midday. The meals always smell and look good. I don't know about the taste, though. I usually get back in time to spoon Thomas's dessert into his mouth.

Now that we're on the subject of food, I must shamefully admit that all of my skirts are getting too tight for me! I was hoping the food here would be revolting and that I'd soon lose weight but not a snowball's hope in Hell!

But there's one thing guaranteed to put you off your food here. You wash your hands before going down to eat, and you're halfway through eating when the fellas from the building site up the road, or down the road, as the case may be, come in early for their lunch, and with a 'Bonjour, bon appétit' stick out a paw to wag your hand. And you're left with millions of little creepies on it. Yuk! It's quite a custom over here, shaking hands, that and the pecks on the cheek!

There's a kid at school called Jean-Christophe whose absolutely gorgeous father brings him to school every morning about half an hour late. I declare to God if I was sitting on the roof JC's father would climb up after me to shake hands!

I'm sure you remember Nolan jabbering on about Johnny Hallyday. Well, everybody is nuts about him over here. He's National Hero No. 1. One day I was late for lunch and ate later with Delphine. Normally we eat the half-hour immediately before the restaurant opens. Well, this day, some of the regulars were eating at the table beside us, and we were sorta talking to them. I asked if JH was married and honestly one fella just gaped at me in open-mouthed astonishment: 'You mean, you don't know what he eats for brekkie every morning?' kinda thing. But then the other fella stood up for me. 'It's not her fault that she's an ignorant twit and doesn't know his life story – she's Irish.'

There was a JH Spectacle on TV one night. He was dressed up with piles of make-up and wore an outfit with chains. Halfway through the programme he had a fight with cavemen carrying *Star Wars* type machine-guns! All of the songs were heavy rock, almost punkish, and, what's more, they were in French! Not my kinda thing. But as Fran and Viv have explained a hundred times since, he was only dressed up like that because it was a 'spectacle' (that is French

– I'm too lazy to look up the English equivalent). Usually, he's much different and much better.

They have piles of his tapes here. The only one of their tapes I like is Elvis's. It's called *Rendezvous avec Elvis*. I believe the English title is simply *Love Songs*. But if you ever get a chance to hear it, take it. It's terrific. I love it and play it as often as possible, which isn't very often. I could rave about it for the next few pages but I've done enough raving for today.

And the reason I'm meanly writing on both sides of the page is because paper like this is like gold. Remember we could never figure out why our penpals always wrote on graph paper? Well, it's because nothing else is sold here.

Wednesday, 5.00 p.m.
Same beach as yesterday

Y'know, the weather here is really changeable. Yesterday, it was so cold and windy and today it's like the middle of July, and I'm not exaggerating. Hopefully, the heat of the sun won't draw the lizards out – it's bad enough being chewed to bits by the flies. I've been assured by both Annique and Vivianne that lizards are 'très gentils' but just looking at them is enough to give me the creeps.

I kept my promise and sang 'Happy Birthday' to you this morning. Myself and Chrystelle were having brekkie; being the last two up, we had the table to ourselves. I suddenly remembered my promise and burst into song; I think Chrys's mouth is still open! I remember <u>my</u> eighteenth birthday; it was all of six months ago. Ooh, the nostalgia of days gone by.

It was just after Sue's party and I was still on Cloud Nine . . .

Well, enough of sentiment and a bit more news. This morning Viv brought me to Concarneau to buy a tennis skirt, as we go to Port Manech every Wednesday to play. There are six courts there and you don't have to pay during the winter months; which is terrific. I got a tour of Port Manech last week and I'm still goggling. It's right on the coast. A <u>very</u> small town, which I believe is exclusively for the rich. You should see the houses. Most of them are sitting on the cliffs like eagles' nests, with a beautiful view of the bay. It's really gorgeous, kinda like Beverly Hills. I should mention that the majority of the houses are summer homes!

The tennis courts are just outside the town and you go down a beautiful tree-lined road to them. Here and there you get a view of the abodes thru the trees – very Castle Park* type, as are the people who live in them, I believe. That seems to be a universal thing, doesn't it?

Well, anyway, we go there for about ninety minutes every Wednesday afternoon. Viv and I both play equally badly, but are improving at an equal rate. She goes every Monday too with François who, I believe, is a very good player. This week Yvan also went with them. He called to the house first and, wow!, my knees are still weak. He was wearing the most fantastic red tracksuit. But, then, on Yvan a flour sack would look fantastic.

(By the way, by devious means I found out that he <u>is</u> married, sob, sob. Chrys is too clever so one day I asked innocent Delphine if Yvan's wife can drive. She said yes and

---

* A private housing estate in Carrick-on-Suir.

that was why he sometimes comes to work on his motorbike – his wife takes the car. Also I asked Chrys what his wife was called as I wanted to send you a sample of Breton names! Clever, eh?)

Well, where was I? Honestly I'm worse than R. L. Stevenson for diversions (it was him who used to divert the whole time in our prose book, wasn't it?).

Oh, yes, in the sportswear shop in Trégunc. Well the fella behind the counter there makes Mark Jennings from *Dynasty* look like Mr Hyde. He's the tennis coach in Trégunc (the fella in the shop, not Mr Hyde!). There was very little left due to the fact that they'll be soon getting their new stock in. I was lucky enough, though, to get a gorgeous tennis dress. It's made of rather clingy material, is mostly white, with blue stripes on the bodice, has two pockets, isn't very short, is closed by fasteners, and is currently covering me, hence the accurate description. But, my God, the price of clothes here is really staggering, no matter what you go to buy. It cost about £22! But a skirt and top would've cost nearly £30. You'd get 'em at home for less than half that. Viv bought a tiny towelling panties to go under her skirt. It cost £8!

There was a good film on last night. It starred Kirk (my hero) Douglas with James Farentino ('Nick Toscanni' from *Dynasty*). *Nimitz*, an aircraft carrier, goes through an electrical storm in mid-Pacific in 1980 and is transported back to the day before Pearl Harbor is attacked (was it the Germans or the Russians that attacked it?). It's fairly good. Also the late film was *Village of the Damned* (y'know *Midwich Cuckoos* by John Whatshisname?). But I was tired and went to bed halfway through it, knowing I'll be able to watch it tonight on the video (great invention, don't you think?).

I suppose I should shut up now and give my tennis arm and your eyes a rest. Please write immediately and let me know how you're getting on AND what Gerard said about me! Be sure and tell your ma and pa I was asking for them. Did Cheryl go to England? Is Anne-Marie working? Is everyone from school keeping in touch? Is there a new biology teacher? Is James Bond on TV every week? Is Miss Carrick really Rose of Tralee? Is the Old Bridge still standing? Is there still a castle in Carrick?

Please write soon.
Tons of love, Catherine

PS Keep me up to date on *Dynasty*!

PPS I don't get the significance of you and Sue making a fuss over my letter to arouse the suspicions of P——. Please explain (if you can). Also, don't try to do the same with this letter as I have a feeling I said something nasty about Sue earlier!

Carrick

Saturday afternoon, 15 October 1983

Dear Cathy,

It's me again! I got your lovely fat letter. Thanks ever so much. Me voici on a really rotten, cold, miserable, windy Saturday (and that's an understatement!). Honestly, the weather here over the past week is really changeable. One day, it's like the Arctic Circle and the next it's like the Mediterranean. I was going to say Italy but I'm so sick of hearing about it from F— over the past weeks. She was there on holliers for three weeks. The people she worked for during the summer brought her out there for nothing. Imagine!

Anyway, since today is Saturday, Aunty Joan was just in. I nearly died laughing with her. You see, Dada and Nanny Gough* have just got in a telephone (yep) and Joan and Teresa† called out to see it in action on Thursday night (they need excitement!). There they all were, gathered round the shining black object in the corner (great material for a thriller, huh?) but nothing was happening. They couldn't get through to anyone. Off went Teresa to the public phone box in Rathgormack promising to phone home (ET-style). In the phone box she asked the operator for Rath 150. By this stage, the excitement being too much, Teresa was in the fits. When the number was answered T burst out 'Tee-hee, Joan, hee-hee, it's me, hee-hee', whereupon this not-too-impressed stern voice bellowed, 'THIS IS NOT JOAN!' and

---

* Mary's maternal grandparents.
† Mary's aunts.

slammed down the receiver. After consultation with the telephone exchange T discovered that (a) Nanny's number was not 150 but 151, and (b) Nanny's telephone wasn't connected to the exchange yet anyway!

Meanwhile, in a little cottage across the fields sat three people intermittently glancing from television to telephone. Suddenly a shrill bell rang. 'There it is,' shouts Nanny, while Dada eyes the phone with mounting trepidation. 'Sit down, ye bloody eejits,' says Joan. 'That's the doorbell on *Terry and June* on the telly.' Nanny declared that she had a pain in her stomach and wished she'd never got the contraption in the first place; Dada moved back his chair and declared that he wouldn't ever go near 'it'. In comes T and explained that the phone wasn't connected properly and that they wouldn't be getting calls for another while (honestly, you'd think there was a fan club ready to bombard 'em). Back they all went to the goggle box, when the clock decided to play a prank – off went the alarm and up jumped Joan to the phone before the whole house became enveloped in roars of laughter. That's all for this week, folks. Tune in next week for another edition of *The Revels of Rathgormack*!

Meanwhile, back to the relative sanity of Carrick and ME. Since I last wrote I started at the WRTC. So now, Kattie chicken, prepare to shield yourself as I prepare to give you a blow by blow (or puff by puff, as I have a cold) account of the goings-on. If you find it heavy going and feel like tearing out your hair (or hairs) with boredom, you have my full permission to omit the next few pages as I rant and rave about it. Yes, I really LOVE it down there.

But first, I'll begin at the beginning. I set off one bright morning (Tuesday, 27 Sept, to be exact) and arrived outside the Garda Barracks in Carrick where I stood waiting for the 7.45 a.m. CIE

Expressway bus. Ber Cooney came along and told me she was travelling too. Anyway, to cut a long story short, I got sick before the bus came. 'Oh, God, here I go again,' says I. Anyway, nothing was going to stop me and I set off for Waterford on the bus. Arriving outside the college I walked up the steps while everyone (waiting outside as the front door was locked) proceeded to goggle. Then I spotted Niamh or should I say we spotted each other. Only then I realised that it was her first day too. She had just come back from holidays the previous day and I needn't tell you I must have looked like death warmed up beside her, me being as sick as a dog an' all.

When the doors opened we sat in the hall while literally hundreds of students began streaming in. Honestly, Cathy, I have never ever seen so many dishy fellas in all my life. While I made my way to powder my nose I got separated from Niamh and that started my search for my class, which continued for the whole morning until dinner time. Honestly, no one behind the desk knew where ACA 1 (my classmates) was. That gives you an insight into the size of the place. I was told by the janitor (a name given to the fellas that hang around looking important even if they're not) to sit outside room D11 until the class (my class) broke up. I did this and, luckily enough, Janette Keevan sat with me for a while as she had no class until after dinner (she's doing music down there). The class broke and – yep, you've guessed it – they weren't my class at all. Anyway, to cut a long story short I finally found them after dinner. I sort of snook in (is there such a word?) but I couldn't get over how friendly everyone was and is.

I think the reason I like WRTC is not my course so much but the class. I was only just thinking that if I was doing a course I liked better then the WRTC would be without fault.

I guess I'll have to tell you about the class so that you can picture my setting. (Catherine Cummins is doing Certified Accountancy and so isn't with me.) My class consists of fourteen girls and twenty-one fellas (go on: turn green) and they're such a zany bunch that I can hardly imagine some of 'em as qualified accountants.

Firstly there's Aidan, who sits in the top right-hand corner all the time. The rest of us change places every day. He hardly mixes at all. I sat beside him one day, and after I'd tried to make conversation without results I gave up. He has a steady girlfriend since Christmas and is so totally wrapped up with her he hardly notices the rest of the world. He's with her every moment of the day, between every class, down in the canteen, just gazing into her eyes. He's really (and I mean really) brainy. He answers all the questions and asks such intelligent ones himself that I don't even understand the question never mind the answer.

Then there's Mairéad, she's very nice but very quiet. Wears glasses too. There's Rita. She's very friendly and always salutes and smiles a lot. There's Majella, who reminds me of Tina Kennedy in character, you know . . . sort of bubbly. There's Margaret who is really quiet and reminds me of Anne Maher in character. Anna is next to her and is very chatty; we had a great chat down in the canteen yesterday. There's Oonagh from Thurles, who is very blunt, which can be hurtful, but she is very down to earth, which I like. There's Bernie from New Ross, who is a bit of a dark horse although I had lunch with her yesterday and found her very nice. There's Nuala who is very . . . sort of suave, she drinks her soup ever so politely, but she's very friendly. Then there's Shane from Limerick who usually sits beside me. He's crazy out but I like him. Then there's Niamh, whom I don't have to describe to you!

The back row consists entirely of fellas who are so witty they made even Tricia Colleton look like an amateur. Honest. They've an answer for everything, which usually leaves me tongue-tied. There's George, whom they're always teasing. There's Maurice, who is absolutely nuts. Himself and Killian sit together and are crazy. They pass all sorts of comments and last week kept imitating hens. You should have heard them. You couldn't help liking Maurice, though. He's sort of boyish (he's <u>only</u> seventeen – just a baby, huh?) and is blond with blue eyes. We had lunch as a crowd a few times in the café in Lisduggan Shopping Centre. We go there instead of the college canteen, which is packed to the hilt. Killian is dark and looks sort of Italian. John is posh and he's got this drawl to match. On the whole he is friendly enough. Then there's Liam, who is <u>the</u> wit of the class. He's really tall and has a cheeky grin which lights up his face. I like him a bit! Then there's Brian, whom we all rag. He was zany the first week but he's quietened down a bit since. He's got lovely deep eyes. There's Mike, who's blond and very friendly.

Then there are two Martins, an unknown fella and a guy called Tony, who's <u>so</u> brainy. There's a girl called Perry, who's brilliant at sketching the teachers. There's Anne and her friend Margaret. There's Dave, who is really nice, from Kilmac, and Niall. There's Joe, who's from Wexford and has the most original accent. I'd like to get to know him better. There's Kay also. Brian Butler from Carrick is there. There are two Eamonns and a Harry, who's a great football player. Finally, there's Robert, the new guy, who's over six feet tall and is the prettiest boy I've ever seen. Honest, 'pretty' is the word. He's sort of punkish and has his dark blond hair highlighted on top. He's a lovely tan and bright blue eyes. So that's all of 'em.

The lecturers are really nice, especially Scott, for Law, who keeps giving brilliant examples of law cases, like the magistrate in England who said, 'As long as I'm sitting in this court prosecuting these blackguards the women of Birmingham can walk the streets in safety.' His classes are really great fun. The classmates are really gas. A lecturer asked us the other day what drisheen* was and a bright spark shouted up, 'What's her second name?'

So all in all I like the Regional except for the long day. I leave home in the dark (at 7.30 a.m.) and come home in the dark (around half six or seven on Friday). You know something, I'll have forgotten what Carrick looks like by next summer!

Talking about Carrick, you wouldn't recognise Pill Road if you saw it now. Remember that farm beside the school with the old stone wall along by the path? Well, that wall is all knocked away as well as the path we used to walk up to school on, down as far as the houses, and you can now see that bungalow from the road (which is being widened).

Now, for some gossip. Are you sitting down? Guess who I heard is pregnant. MRS DENNY. All Greenhill is agog with it. Y— and D— are getting married next Saturday. Martin is invited to a do afterwards in the Bess. Ma bought 'em a pressie. I heard that T— is selling soup from door to door. Imagine, six hons and you end up selling soup! Anne-Marie frightened the life on me. She had been given a ring as a present from Angela and she had me convinced that she was engaged. She kept it up for hours, she did. I nearly killed her when she owned up. Bang went my hopes of being bridesmaid!

I suppose you know by this stage that Anne is in St Joseph's

---

* A type of black pudding.

doing domestic science. I saw B— T— down at the WRTC. She goes around with this gang and you always hear her before you see her. I also met Karen. She snubbed me for a whole two weeks until I finally met her in the canteen. She hadn't recognised me at all! We go to the canteen all the time instead of the library. By the way, Niamh got thrown out of the latter for talking (tee-hee, tee-hee)!

I'm glad you're getting on with the kids. You're really lucky. I met Sue's mother over town about two weeks ago (or rather she met me; she nearly backed me into a shop window, honest). She was agog about you getting Journalism or sommat. Is that true? She went on and on about you going to France. Needless to say I stood up for you and said you were right. I was nearly going to say that you'd probably turn out 100 times better than college graduates but I remembered who I was talking to in time. Fair dues to you, Kitty chicken! She then convinced me that Sue got five honours since an A in Irish counted for two.

The new season clothes in the shops are gorgeous but unfortunately I can't afford 'em. Cheryl did go to England but she's back now minding her cousin's baby. She comes over some nights and is also learning typing in the Tech on Monday night. (I'm answering your questions now.) The new biology teacher is . . . FEMALE (aw, shucks!). James Bond is on TV every week, yep.

About Miss Carrick, her name is Brenda Hyland. She isn't from Carrick and you are mixing her up with the Festival Queen. I've sent you the picture of Brenda as Rose of Tralee.

Well, that's about all is happening around here. I'm enjoying the Regional but I don't feel at all sure about accountancy. The others seem to like it. Some have a business background and that makes it easier. They're also <u>really</u> brainy.

Uncle Paddy was in today. The telly was on with *Tarzan* and black African chiefs on horses. Paddy asks in a loud innocent voice, 'Where's the racing from today?' Ma had to dive out into the back kitchen to stop him from seeing her laughing.

Well, Kitty, I'm gonna shurrup because I'm running out of words and I gorra pain in me 'and. Goodbyeeeeee! You'd better write soon.

Lots of love,
Mary

PS I can't tell you what is happening in *Dynasty* because the new season hasn't started yet! No one got killed in the *Dallas* fire (aw, shucks). See ya.

(By the way, Vera, Teresa Fogarty, Anne Cullinane, Rosie Flynn and a pile more are below in the college too!)

(Who says I'll never write a novel!)

Trégunc

Monday, 17 October 1983

Remember how crazy we were about Peter Strauss when we were in sixth class? Well, I found this photograph and accompanying interview in *Téléstar* the French version of the *RTÉ Guide*. I wonder if we've changed that much in five years. Only for the fact that his name is there in block capitals, I wouldn't believe that it was the same person, would you?

Also included is a tiny example of some French programmes. Personally I prefer the comic strip! I'm sure that you also remember Nolan blabbing about Julien Clerc? So, hopefully, you'll appreciate the little piccy of him too. I've seen him once on telly. And, boy, is he gorgeous! His smile has the same effect as that of Michael! (As a singer he isn't bad either!) If you look on the back, you'll see a shot from *Cabaret*, which I saw last week. It was very good, but I'm glad that Nanny wasn't in the room! I've a feeling that RTÉ showed it last year but I'm not sure. Anyway, if you get a chance it's worthwhile watching, even if you only watch Michael York!

I suppose that you're wondering why I'm blabbing on in this fashion ('Don't you always blab on in that fashion?' says you!!!). Well, you see, last night I helped myself to Viv's typewriter; and now I cannot stop using it!!! So, I'm writing bits of letters to everybody, even though I don't owe anybody a letter. You're lucky, though, I wrote to Sue last night but it was only today that I found the way to make capital letters. Also last night, the only punctuation I was capable of was commas and exclamation marks!!

I have to shut up for the moment as it's time to go to school again to collect Thomas; also I have to give another English lesson. At the moment, everybody can say 'poor little dog' and 'poor little cat'. The kids are surprisingly good. please excuse the fact that this paragraph is even worse than the other ones. But you see I'm listening to a Joan Baez record as well as typing and if you know anything about her you'll know that you should really give her songs your full attention. anyway, must go for now, ciao. (That's Italian for 'au revoir', which is French for 'goodbye', which is English for 'slán leat', which is the end of this PS as I've run out of languages!)

PS The reason I only type this part of the letter is because when you type with six fingers, it's really slow, and you cannot write and think about what you want to say so freely. Consequently, when I type, my letters are more restrained and not as spontaneous. Well, ya can't have it all ways, can ya? Write soon.

Thursday, 20 October

♪♪ I wanna go home, I wanna go home, Oh Lord, I wanna go home! ♪♪

Dear Mary,
Thanks a million for your package, which arrived today. You're an angel for sending the photo of the castle. I wanted to ask someone to do so, so that I could show it off here!

Anyway, I've been feeling really depressed lately; and while your letter cheered me up, it also increased my depression somewhat. Y'see, I also got a letter from Sue today and there's the two of you blabbing on about all your new copains et copines and I've met absolutely nobody since I last wrote; excuse me, since the day I arrived. Now, you know what a likeable, friendly, outgoing, cheerful person I am, and this loneliness is driving me absolutely out of my mind.

But I love the descriptions enclosed. They sound a really great bunch (hence the song on the top of the page!). Also from what I can make out there isn't any of the boy-girl shyness. Please keep me in the news as to all of the class goings-on, as I need to be cheered up.

Has your grandma put up a toll-booth at her gate, in order to charge local cavemen for looking at her talking machine? Please tell her and the aunts I was asking for them, although I doubt that they remember me. If I'm alone here when the phone rings, I just keep my fingers crossed and wait for it to stop! It's hard enough trying to speak French face-to-face with somebody, but on the phone . . .

Viv and François went to Paris last Monday. They're doing up their old apartment in order to sell it. When they came to Brittany four years ago they rented it; and I believe the tenants did a bit of redecorating! So, Delphine and Thomas are staying with their grandma in Trégunc while I stay here with Chrys.

So, as you can imagine, this week has been really boring. Mind you, there's plenty of ironing to do. Viv didn't ask me to do it. But if I don't, I feel guilty that I'm not earning my keep (£25 p.w.). Also when I'm here in the house by myself, I love dusting and little things like that, imagining that it's my own house . . . Some people never grow up, do they?!

But over the past week, I've gotten to know Chantal, Bruno and Yvan a <u>tiny</u> bit better. As you probably know I'm fundamentally shy (pull the other one . . .) and so never talk when there's a big crowd at the table. Four is friendlier and so I sometimes venture a comment. On Monday afternoon I went playing tennis with Yvan for an hour. He isn't great at tennis but just the same is better than me. But I think the reason I played so badly was because I kept watching him and not the tennis balls! Did I tell you before that he's absolutely gorgeous, and has lovely smiley eyes, and beautiful white teeth and a devastating smile and a terrific voice and a wife and a three-year-old son? Well, even if I did, he's worth two mentions (okay, so it's a bit too long to be described as a mention but what the heck!).

I hope to God you're right about Denny, because I'm going to send her a 'Congratulations' card. Anyway, Sue also imparted the same news. So if it isn't true, I'll just have to kill the two of you! As well as all of that, I nearly forgot, I had a letter from Reggie on Wednesday. She chatted away for four pages, then put on her veil and picked up her rosary beads, proceeding to warn me about rushing into marriage and letting boys get their own selfish way and letting them use me. If it wasn't so funny (boys being a bit thin on the ground in this corner of the world) I'd be quite annoyed at her.

My sympathies on your confrontation with Sue's mam, who really isn't such a bad old thing ('Easy for you to say,' says you!), but she is right about me getting an interview for journalism in Dublin. I was also told that I'd been accepted for a laboratory technician's course in Kevin Street. But by the time Nanny had forwarded the form to me it was far too late to reply. I felt positively sick for a whole week at myself. Even now I have a green tinge! I'd have loved to have done journalism, but I'm absolutely positive that the phrase 'The other man's grass . . .' was coined for me.

Late at night when the wind's howling around the eaves (the weather's broken!), I lie awake in my bed, listening to Chrys and the dog snoring in the bed across the room (achoo, achoo!) and worry that in fifty years' time I'm going to be old and withered with a life wasted looking after kids and letting my brains go to rack and ruin. Further chilling chapters of this horrendous tale next week.

I've discovered Viv's classical music collection. I just adore Mozart's 40th Symphony and 'Petite Musique de Nuit'. Please listen to them sometime. They really are lovely!

Please excuse the interruption . . . I hopped out to buy a bag of sweets (tut, tut, tut!). Also, I had to turn the record over. Made some coffee to keep the chill out of these old bones!

Are you keeping in touch with Sue? Had a letter from A—. She says she's given up because of the way she goes on about college the whole time. She seems to be having a whale of a time in Limerick and her classmates and roommates sound terrific. Like you, she's been lucky. She went to a disco one night and seems to have had a great time. She's lucky she has Gerard there. Also, I think she's still stuck on C—, poor Sue!

As I already said Mme and M. are in Paris and return tomorrow, I think. So, there are just four of us for lunch every day. At night, the restaurant being closed, Chrys and I eat in the house. But anyway, today was very funny. Somehow or another the subject got around to Christmas. Bruno asked me if I was spending it in France, whereupon I said, 'No, I'm going to go to London, I think, to Celia or Daddy.' But I told them I hadn't mentioned it to Viv yet. So Yvan did an impression of Viv getting up one morning and finding a note from me saying, 'Gone to London, see you next week!' Not only is he very good-looking, he's also extremely witty! (He showed me how to use a microwave today! Swoon! How romantic! You'd never think he was married, you know. He never mentions her or the kid. And never seems to be in a hurry to get home. Most peculiar! I haven't got a crush on him or anything like that. I just like him as a person and not as a male. So, please don't get any wrong ideas. I'm definitely not – unfortunately – a femme fatale!)

Where was I? Oh, yes, Christmas. Well, you see the thing is the restaurant will most likely be open on Xmas Eve. That means the three of them will have to work. It might even be open 25 Dec. So they started cheering when I said I wouldn't be here. They're perceptive, y'see! No au-pair – who's going to look after the kids if Mommy and Daddy are working, huh? But then, being the killjoy that I am, I told them that last year the kids went to stay with their uncle! Hee-hee! You should have seen their faces drop!

I've been feeling really lazy lately and have barely been out walking at all. As well as that, the weather hasn't been exactly favourable. You look out the window, see a lovely blue sky, on with your coat, open the door and it's raining! And honestly, I'm not exaggerating. François was supposed to fix up Chrys's bike for me about six weeks ago but it's still as flat as a pancake!

Speaking of which, we had crêpes for supper one night. While being gorgeous, I've tasted nicer things – pizza, for example! By this stage even my watch and earrings are getting too tight for me!

I didn't see the postman, but Chantal did and she says he wants to know if I'd give his daughter English grinds. Yippee! A few more bob for Canada and Paris! (Ask Sue or Catherine about my plans for Canada and Paris!)

I love teaching English at school. The kids are really smart and pick up things so quickly. I'm alternatively called 'Anglaise', 'Catherine', 'Maîtresse' and 'Irlandaise'. Quite a variety, huh?

How are your parents? Are they happy that you are going to WRTC? I'm sure that you make the two of them feel ten feet high. And that isn't false praise.

WARNING: My hitherto perfect writing is going to deteriorate from here as Mimique, feeling lonely (achoo!), has decided to honour me by sitting (ow!) in my lap. French cats have very long claws. How are your adopted moggies keeping?

I think when Viv comes home tomorrow I'll ask her about night school in Trégunc and Concarneau. That way I might learn how to type properly and at the same time meet some people my own age.

I'm more or less running out of news now. Please write back soon and let me know how life is treating you. And don't forget to say who said what, and who smiled at you, etc., in WRTC. Catherine sent me a description of her accountancy lecturers, who sound a great bunch especially Albert Keating. Have you got any in common with her?

Thanks for the *Opinion*, which I'm going to read, curled up at the fire – sorry, radiator – tonight.

Really must dash. WRITE SOON.
Tons of love,
Catherine

PS Say 'hello' to Maw and Paw for me.

PPS Have you been sick since going to Waterford? And have you found out what's causing it? Is it just nerves or what? Have you met any of the people from the factory in New St? I heard B— is out of work again.

Carrick

Tuesday, 1 November 1983

Dear Cathy,

It's me again (that kind, caring, cheerful, generous, modest soul from 63). Anyway, I gets the impression you ain't too happy with yourself. Well, join the club. Honest, I've just plunged into a fit of depression myself. 'Okay,' says you, 'what about the WRTC?'

Well, what about it? Needless to say, the novelty has worn off – and now I see I've made the biggest mistake of my whole life. Don't get me wrong, I really like going there better than anything else. It's funny but I feel a sense of identity just going there. I've stopped getting sick by the way. I think it was just nerves. But to get back to what I was saying, the fact is I haven't made any real friends at all (stress the real). There are a few reasons for this.

Firstly, I've come to the conclusion that I'm too serious and shy. I just can't let go somehow. The crack is great but I seem to be enjoying it from the outside without actually taking part. I mean, every time someone says something witty to me, I'm just lost for words and I end up looking like a snobby swot. Last week, for example, one of the guys came in and all the other guys started teasing him about a date he had the night before. Jokingly they were asking him what he did. He said he had kept his hands to himself whereupon they started ragging him. Suddenly, he turned to me and said, 'Do you think I'm gay?' Well, you can imagine my face. If it had been somebody else they'd have thought of something witty to say, but not me. At least if you get dumbstruck you can blame the language barrier!

Dear Cathy,

It's me again (th[e]
kind, caring, cheerful, generou[s]
modest soul from 63)
Anyway, I gets the impre[ssion]
you ain't too happy with
[w]ell join the club. Hones[t]
[j]ust plunged into a fit
[of] depression myself. Okay
[n]ow what about the WR[...]
Well, what about it? N[...]
[to] say the novelty has [...]
[o]ff — and now I see I'v[e]
[m]ade the biggest mistake
[m]y whole life. Don't get
[wr]ong, I really like [it]
[h]ere better than anyt[hing]
[els]e. It's funny but I [...]
sense of identity just [...]
[be]ing there. I've storeed [...]

I suppose then again I'm more conservative than most of the students. One fella in our class didn't go to bed until five o'clock for three mornings in a row. Guess what he was doing – playing poker in his digs. And here was I thinking I was bad with a few games of 'Over the Top' and 'Snap'! The Students' Union are selling contraceptives in the shop.* The class reps were asked to pass the message around. You can imagine the wisecracks that were made when poor Shane had to announce it from the top of the class. Coming home on the bus one evening, there was a guy smoking pot in front of me. I was nearly high and me only sitting behind him!

Thirdly, I don't stay in digs so that sort of hampers friendship-making. All the rest of 'em are in clubs together. On Wednesday night there was a Hallowe'en Ball. A good few of the class went and didn't get in until 4.30 a.m. You should have seen 'em on Thursday. Michael had a king-size hangover and spent the whole day going out for fresh air. Lastly, there's Niamh. You see, we seem to go everywhere together (even to the Ladies!).

As well as that a good few of the class are 'bourgeoisie' (or should I say bore-geoisie!). One day I nearly fell asleep at the lunch break as a few of 'em discussed the merits of a Triumph Spitfire over an Austin something-or-other. Now you know me, Cathy, I haven't even gorra rusty bike and here they were going on about Daddy's Merc and Mummy's Jag and how they'd learnt to drive and who they were insured with and . . . yawn, yawn, yawn. Another day it was all about holidays. Not for them the Ring of Kerry or Ballybunion. It was all the South of France and Spain and

*In Ireland in 1983 contraceptives (including condoms) could only be dispensed by a pharmacist on presentation of a doctor's prescription. That's why I was shocked to see condoms on sale in the college shop – it was illegal!

Switzerland, etc. And there was I whose only holidays were in Glen Lower and Ballypatrick! So you see I usually just sit there trying not to yawn or get sick or both!

On the whole, though, I enjoy the college experience, especially travelling – I've met some really nice people on the buses. But again they're merely acquaintances and not true friends. One thing all of this has taught me is how valuable our friendship is and that's why I'm sending you a boat to come home for Christmas. (Okay, it's only a folded paper one but maybe if you cut down on the sweets you'll manage it! Talking about sweets, I've never eaten so many as I have lately. You should see my skin. Even as I write this I'm chewing KitKat.)

Come to think of it I might be expelled tomorrow. Yep, EXPELLED! You see, the VEC aren't paying the college fees to the school until January and the principal below in WRTC is broke and wants us to pay the fees now. But if we do, the VEC won't refund us the money so the Students' Union has advised us not to pay (anyway, I haven't 220 pence at the moment, never mind pounds). Well, the principal sent around letters last week saying that if we hadn't paid by tomorrow we will have to 'discontinue' our studies there. The Students' Union have vowed to go on strike if anyone is thrown out. Just think . . . by the time you get this I might be ploughing up and down the Cork Road with my placard shouting nasty things about Gemma the Hussey!*

Last Sunday, myself, Eleanor and Sue went on the Macra Treasure Hunt (in cars) out your way. It was really <u>great</u> fun. Sue left her bike at the guards' barracks and since it began to rain in the evening she got a lift home. Martin had to call for the bike.

* Education minister.

Sue's mother called up for it on Saturday. You know, I never noticed before the way she ignores remarks about Sue but brings in Ger instead. For instance, I asked her did Sue get home okay. She said, 'She did, but Tommy had to go for Gerard because his bike got punctured.' When my mother asked did Sue have a cover for her saddle she said, 'Oh, Gerard's got one all right. He keeps his bike carefully.' When I admired the jumper Sue was wearing on Saturday and asked if she had knitted it, she said, 'I did, but you should have seen the beautiful silver-grey one I knitted for Gerard. It's only gorgeous.' I never really noticed this before, have you?

By the way, I got an invitation to a wedding. No, it's not Anne-Marie's but Shawn's.* Yep, in comes this envelope with an invitation in it – no letter or nothing. Out fell a piece of paper. 'Oh, goodie,' says I, 'she's sent the ticket as well!' Wishful thinking! It was only a scrap of tissue paper. (Anyway, I ain't going, though I'd really love to.) Talking about paper, don't worry about what sort of paper you write on, I'd read your writings even if they were written on loo paper!

How's your tennis going? (or should I say where are the tennis balls going?)

Hope you enjoy the *Carrick Opinion*.

And now for another episode of *The Revels of Rathgormack*. The black object is working and strange voices can be heard coming through the wires. Anyway, Nanny finally got through to Johnny (one of the brood across the water). 'Hello, son,' says she. 'This is Mother,' whereupon the rest of them went into convulsions because Nanny always called herself 'Mama' before going all mod. Daddy Gough picked up the receiver and, after

* Mary's American penpal.

shouting the weather forecast into the wrong end, proceeded to exclaim to all and sundry what a marvellous invention it was!

Listen, I'd better go. Mamaw wants to visit the cemetery because she wants a plenary indulgence for all of her sins but she's afraid of the ghosties so I have to hold her hand! She tells me to tell you that the coffee-table is still in the corner. (I bet you're the only person to have a coffee-table as a monument!)

Cheryl went for an interview for AnCO for a secretarial course. She'll have to go for another one after that. Listen, Maw's having kittens so I'd better go.

All my love, God bless and for heaven's sake, kid, keep that chin up. Be a proud Irish gal!

XX Mary

PS You'd better write soon.

Trégunc

Monday, 7 November 1983

Dear Mary,

You said you wouldn't mind if I wrote on loo paper – so here goes! As you can see, it's really quite legible – well, as legible as my writing will ever be, that is! However, as you will discover if you endeavour to copy me, one must be extremely careful, as this particular type of stationery is rather fragile and tends to disintegrate under pressure.

PTO

Due to that fact, I've replaced the rest of the roll back where it belongs, and where it will serve equally as important a purpose as the notepaper with which I'm going to finish this encyclical.

Okay?

Love always,
Catherine

Dear Mary,

Thanks for your little parcel, which arrived yesterday while I was at Quimper. Boy, were you down in the dumps when you wrote it! If I remember I was in the same type of humour the last time I tried to blind you! However, I've cheered up considerably since then, and black depression rarely hits me – only once or twice a day!

Well, what's been happening since the last time? Oh, yeah,

there was a week's mid-term break. Franck, one of the Parisian cousins, was here for ten days or so. He's only twelve but you'd think he was our age, and I'm really not exaggerating. He's terribly nice – an absolute nut!

I'm fairly sure I mentioned my visit to Paris for February to you? Well, thanks to Franck, I got a bit more info on my guide. Y'see, he's a very good friend of Franck's family – a kinda adopted uncle, I believe. From what I can figure out he's twenty-three-ish, smokes eighty cigarettes a day (my poor lungs!), is an ardent Communist, and loves discussing this subject. He works in the Mairie (town hall) with Annie, Viv's sister, and is taking his holidays at the same time as her, just to have the honour of showing me around! Generous, huh!

I'm really looking forward to going, though. If you remember I always wanted to visit Paris. I think that goes back to third class and Sister Marie Antoinette, who was the first to introduce me to the guillotine and Revolution and so on.

And speaking of the Revolution, Mary, I made a disappointing discovery relating to it last week. You know it was all about Liberty, <u>Equality</u> and Fraternity and so on. But in their own way, they're just as snobbish and class-regulated now as they were when Marie-Antoinette suggested everybody eat cake! 'What the hell is this unbearably long, winding paragraph leading to?' says you. 'Well,' says me, 'it's all this dreadfully complicated tutoyer-ing and vouvoyer-ing that they have over here.' And if I hadn't taken your dictionary you'd be able to look it up and discover that those words refer to the fact that certain people are addressed as 'tu' and others as 'vous'. Sure, I know Nolan mentioned it, but rather briefly. And the French use 'vous' about 90 per cent of the time! I mean practically everyone is referred to as 'vous'. Even in many families the parents are called 'vous' by their children. Awful, isn't it?

Viv was saying that they'd told the people in the restaurant to say 'tu' to her and the rest of the family. But no go! They stick to the more formal one. I've kept my ears open over the past week and am pleased to report that they say 'tu' to me! 'Vous' is considered to be a mark of respect but I don't think I consider it so. Well, enough of this boring French lesson! Just keep it in mind when you visit this neck of the woods.

Almost forgot! Guess what I had for supper on Sunday night! Yep, you've got it! Those slimy creepy-crawlies with shells on their backs. And, boy, were they gorgeous! And as I've told you a million times before, I don't exaggerate! Really, though, they taste lovely, and are served with a terrific sauce. François came out of the kitchen and presented me with a plate with the escargots on it. He told me to eat it, and afterwards he'd tell me what it was. Well, now, Molly dear, y'know what a bright spark I am. So I chirps up, helping myself at the same time, 'Them there's snails, no?' (In French, of course.) I was surprised, though. The next time you go to the Central Grill you should order them! (Please get someone to film the waitress's face and send a copy of it to me!)

Unfortunately, I've been promised Kermit's little footsy-wootsies next week. And that I'm not really looking forward to. But then I suppose there really isn't much difference between frogs and snails. But to tell you the truth I've always been petrified of frogs since a boy – I think it was Paul Healy! – chased me with one in High Babies.

Oh, yes, an example of François's sense of humour. We had rabbit for supper one night. As he spooned the accompanying carrots onto my plate he explained that as rabbits eat carrots when they're alive it's considered good taste to serve that particular vegetable with them when they're dead, funny, eh? Bet Bugs Bunny doesn't think so!

And while I think of it, I'm in very bad humour with you. You didn't send me a bit of news in your letter, ya nit-wit, ya! Hence I am dying to know if Denny is or isn't. And you never said! Also not a word about any mutual acquaintances; well, admittedly you mentioned a few!

On the other hand, I'm very grateful for the *Carrick Opinion*. But, my God, the price of the stamp! Look, I know how tough it is on you poor students (are you still a student?) so, if you like, mutilate the paper and send me the relevant bits. I'll suffer in silence. There's no point in throwing away your money like that. But then, let's face reality, money spent on ME is NEVER wasted, now, is it?

Speaking of money, myself and Vivianne went to Quimper (it's on the map, look it up!) yesterday on a bit of a shopping spree. We were supposed to start at around 9 a.m. but by the time we (well, truthfully, she!) were ready to go, it was after ten o'clock. I went down to the restaurant just before we left, and got a wolf-whistle from Bruno, who is rather tight with that commodity! A real lift for the spirits! Remember the sky-blue trousers I got in Mirror Mirror? I wore them with a pair of navy leg warmers that I knitted, as well as my navy jumper and bright red shoes.

Well, where was I? Oh, yeah, Viv had something to do in Nevez, Trégunc and Concarneau, in that order. Got to Trégunc, went to the bank, came back to the car, and the blinking thing wouldn't start. I felt like crying, as we were supposed to go to Quimper twice before that, but each time something cropped up.

Well, anyway we walked to the garage a kilometre up the road; mechanic gave us a lift back to Trégunc, belted the engine with his hammer and, hey presto, no more trouble!

So, anyway, it was nearly twelve when we got to Quimper. Viv had to do a bit of business for the restaurant, something to do with the bookkeeping aspect. Then, we'd the rest of the day to ourselves.

The city is really, absolutely truthfully, gorgeous. It's just won a prize as France's most beautifully flowered town. That translation isn't terrific, but I'm sure you know what I mean. The streets are cobbled and the shops go back to the Middle Ages. Not all of them, of course. The cathedral is breath-taking both inside and out. At the risk of giving me grandmother a heart attack, I'll have to criticise the richness of the Catholic Church. And I'm not speaking of spiritual richness either! I said something to that effect to Vivianne yesterday, and she said to me, 'Yet you go to Mass every Sunday!' (At Mass, I'm the only one who hasn't grey hair or milk teeth, if you know what I mean. The church attendance rate here seems to be worse than the Irish one. End of diversion, back to Quimper.)

After lunch we spent ages in this huge shop specialising in material. I want to make nightdresses for the twins for Christmas. Also, I bought some white cotton to make myself a Slavic-type blouse with embroidery.

Then Viv spotted a pair of shoes that she liked. She'd tried for the same type everywhere from Paris to Trégunc with no success. So in she goes to the shop and wow! My mouth is still open. It was a place where they sold all leather and leather-related stuff. You should have seen the dresses. Absolutely gorgeous, and the belts and the shoes and the bags and the prices!

Well, Viv bought her shoes. They're black, like dolly shoes but in leather, and have a tiny ankle strap – £35! And we complain at home about the price of stuff.

On the way back to the car park, we started looking in the boutique windows. (I don't think 'started' is a good choice of verb as we'd been doing that all day!) So, she spotted a lovely dress. In she goes, tries on a half-dozen, and emerges with a gorgeous grey skirt and blouse. I cannot describe the material very well, but it's like a hyper-soft leather or something. That cost around £150.

Now you may get the idea that she does nothing but buy clothes. Well, that isn't true. She's never bought anything for herself since I've arrived. Also, she holds onto things. For example, the last time she bought herself a coat, she was pregnant with Delphine who's 7½ now! But when she does get something, it's good quality.

So, after all that, I stumbled in the door last night at around six o'clock with aching feet and bulging arms to be greeted by your letter. What's Chris de Burgh's album called? *At the End of a Perfect Day.*

Last week, I went to the hairdresser in Port Manech. I got it cut quite short with very little layering and a flick. It's quite difficult, though, to keep the flick! The place is run by a girl and a boy. I was quite surprised when I saw the guy at first. But I nearly had heart failure when I saw the bill – IR£11.50. It'd have cost about £5 in Hairport. Can you imagine what a perm'd cost over here?

Unlike you, I'm going to answer a few questions that you posed in your letter!

The subject of Gerard . . . I must admit I copped on ages and ages ago that he's Mummy's favourite. Hadn't you? Go and get your goggles changed! He's her No. 1 topic of conversation. In fact I'd go as far as saying that he's her only topic of conversation. But to tell you the truth it was only after Joan got to know Sue's mother that I really noticed. Joan copped on immediately and remarked upon it to me. Then I too began to keep all my eyes and ears open.

But I'm sure you've noticed by this stage that Sue herself does the same thing. No matter what you're talking about she finds some way of dragging Gerard in. Cast your mind back to when we first knew Sue – I mean we got to know Sue and Gerard at the same time, didn't we, despite the fact that neither of us met him for, what, three or four years?

I doubt that you'll get the wrong impression about what I think of Gerard, but better safe than sorry, I suppose, so I'll keep on going for a few more paragraphs about him! (God, wouldn't I love to be sitting with you in the Grill or ice-cream parlour and be able to talk with my mouth instead of my pen!)

Despite the fact that Sue has been singing his praises since I first knew her, I haven't been turned off him. Of course there were times when I got fed up of hearing about him and longed to tell her to shut up. After I first met him, though –

summer 1982, I think – it wasn't so boring, as I was able to give her my own opinion about him too. D'you understand what I'm trying to say? I've a feeling I didn't say it too clearly!

You probably felt the same way? But despite the fact that the whole family have him on a pedestal, and try to carry out his every wish before he even utters it, he's not in the least bit spoilt-brattish or nasty or all other similar descriptions. In fact, I'm probably repeating myself: he's one of the nicest <u>persons</u> I know. Please note the underlining and leave Cupid out of this.

AND FOR THE THIRD TIME, WHAT DID YOU TWO SAY THAT NIGHT OUTSIDE YOUR GARDEN GATE (WITH ALL THE NEIGHBOURS PEEPING OUT THE WINDOWS) ABOUT ME? YOU KNOW YOU'RE GOING TO TELL ME SOMETIME SO WHY NOT NOW? I NEED SOME CHEERING UP (EM . . . WILL IT CHEER ME UP?) BUT PLEASE JUST GIVE US SOME CLUE – PLEASE.

I've got a heck of a pain in my hand, so I'll have to shut up soon. Mind you . . . I've had the pain since page 4. Hey, ya never filled me in on the details of your eighteenth birthday. Please do so!

As of yet, I haven't had a chance to discuss Christmas with Vivianne. I'm waiting for a suitable opportunity to present itself. But I'm getting a bit homesick now and I miss all the lads* from school more than I thought I would! I really want to go home for 25 Dec.

So yesterday I manoeuvred Delphine into asking why you'd sent the little paper boat. Viv was nearby and I said the boat was to bring me home for Christmas! Smart, huh! But

* Girls.

I'm going to say it to her soon and put an end to all of this uncertainty!

I think I'd better sign off, before me paw falls off! I hope your maw's keeping me monumental coffee-table shined up! Tell both your parents that I was asking for them, won't you?

Be sure and write soon.

Lots of love,
Catherine

PS When *Dynasty* starts keep me informed, won't you? Also, I'm thinking very seriously of taking up a correspondence course here which lasts for nineteen months. I have sent away for info. I should have settled for definite by the next time I write.

PPS ♪♪ Pack up your troubles in your old kit bag and smile, smile, smile ♪♪ In other words 'chin up' and don't worry.

If you're still gracing WRTC with your presence, let me know how life is going there. Also, why didn't you say to whatshisname, 'I've always found you very cheerful, but gay would be a bit of an exaggeration!' I can just see you going up to him saying, 'Remember last month you asked me if I thought you were gay, well . . .'

Any idea what Hally's* doing? What's the new biology teacher like? Is Pepper† improving any, and is Goofy‡ still as nosy as ever?

* Miss Hallinan, our former Irish teacher.
† Sister Perpetua, the new principal of our former secondary school.
‡ Sister de Porres, Sister Perpetua's predecessor.

Remington Steele is starting here on Sunday afternoons at 2.30 p.m. But I doubt that I'll get to see much of it with the kids! Anyway, Sunday afternoons I go to the beach to watch the wind-surfing.

Have only had one letter from Anne Maher so far. Have completely given up on her! Weather is terrific at the moment. There was even a woman swimming last Sunday! And, what's more, she wasn't wearing the top of her bikini!

Please excuse the untidiness of all these extra notes that I've suddenly remembered. But I'm not going to go upstairs again for my notepaper!

Carrick

Sunday, 27 November 1983

How ya, Kitty,

It's meself is in it. You must be wondering where I was all this time but the truth is your letter was late coming. 'Now,' sez I, 'what's happened to my friend, my bosom pal even? Have the French froggies taken their toll?' I was on the point of engaging Sherlock Holmes (or his equivalent) to solve the mystery of the missing Kitty when along came your letter!

Seriously, though, your letter was a breath of fresh air. Anyway, a thousand apologies for the dismal down-heartedness of the last letter. This one will be better (sez you, 'Anything would be an improvement').

Well, any road, I'm still gracing WRTC with my presence (as you so aptly put it). Actually I was nearly in trouble last week. Twelve of us were called to Mr Merriman's office (you should hear what he's called) for not paying the college fees yet. Was I telling you that I also got a letter from Griffin (the principal) saying if I didn't pay up I'd be out? Anyway, we had to go up three at a time. Robert (the good-lookin' punk) and Kay were with me. I went in half expecting to be thrown out on the spot but he was very nice. I had to explain to him that although the others' grants had come through, mine hadn't yet and so I couldn't afford to pay 220 quid. Honestly, I felt <u>so</u> small as he told me not to be ashamed, that I could pay in instalments. Imagine! I felt like some second-class citizen. Any notion I had of the equality of education services in this country is eternally banished. Believe me, most of the students in my class are rolling in the green. Some of them would sicken you with the talk of cars, clothes and money, money, money. Come to think of it, I think I'll ask Santa for ear plugs. If I don't I'm in real danger of becoming an inverted snob!

Tut, tut. I must not be nasty, I must not be nasty, I must not be nasty.

Anyway, Maw and Paw have been decorating the ould homestead. The living room (seems too extravagant a word for this here place of eating, drinking, watching telly and other pastimes too numerous to mention) has been wallpapered in a beige paper and new lino has been put down. She got a carpet for the master bedroom (the MASTER's bedroom!). She conned the poor salesman into cutting his price from £80 down to £28. Honestly, I ask you, how can anyone cut his profit margin by that much (unless it fell off the back of a truck in the first place)? I firmly believe that Maw could sell oil to the Arabs (or, should I say, persuade them to give it to her for nuttin'). The carpet is brown. The lino in the living room is browny tan. She also papered the loo in a brown beige paper. AND, KITTY CHICKEN, I DO DECLARE IF SHE BRINGS ANYTHING ELSE INTO THE HOUSE THAT'S BROWN, I'M BUYING A TENT AND MOVING OUT. AND YOU CAN GUESS WHAT COLOUR THE TENT WON'T BE.

Another thing, I firmly believe the age of chivalry is dead. Last Monday morning I had to stand all the way from Carrick to Waterford. Every one of the strapping young males remained glued to their seats. Any ideas of being a femme fatale have gone out the window. I also got two doors swung in my face last Friday. Now I ask you, Kitty, is that any way to treat a lady? Those damned women's libbers and their equality agenda have ruined all hopes of chivalry. We can't have it both ways, I know. But I still think they were a lousy bunch of so-and-sos. I mean, I wouldn't slam a door in a fella's face, would I?

How's your typing coming along? Are you going to night classes? By the way, who is Annique, and I meant to ask you how did you start teaching English in the first place? Is Anne still the apple of your eye? You know something, Cathy, that was one thing that surprised me – the way you settled in with the kids. I mean, don't get me wrong, I don't think you're Attila the Hun or anything ... but seriously, I thought you had a distaste for all them there varmints. I'm really delighted for you. I mean, after all, it'd be terrible to turn your back on those female motherly instincts, eh?

(There goes the funeral bell for S—'s grandfather. He got a terrible death from cancer.)

Anyway, to finally put you out of your misery about what Gerard said ... I can't because I've forgotten most of what he said. I mean, you hardly think he'd say anything memorable about an insignificant creature like you, would you, old chappie?! Seriously, though, most of what he said was an in-depth study of your character. He said you were very brave to go abroad on your own. I said something about you being confident or at least giving that impression. And wait for it – he said he thought you were as self-conscious as anybody else but you were good at hiding any insecurity. I never thought he'd be so observant, would you? That was about the gist of it but I can tell you something for nothing: he seems to have a very high regard and respect for you. Play your cards right, Kitty, and you never know ...

Sue and I didn't rejoin Macra this year. I haven't the money actually. I saw John this morning. He put up his hand as I passed the car and I had to stop my mouth from popping open. I wonder will he be at Sue's party this year. Will you ever forget last year – me getting stuck with the seatbelt in his car an' all? Oh, Gawd, the embarrassment – I'm blushing at the thought. I don't propose to be any more sophisticated now but I hope to God I never find myself in a situation like that again. Remember 'A Winter's Tale'? I heard it lately and I got all reminiscent, remembering your crush and the lack of outcome. Isn't it great, Cathy, being where we are (age-wise, I mean)? I really enjoy being eighteen 'cos you have a degree of independence and yet you can act the gom if you want 'cos we're not 'all growed up' yet. Without sounding corny, I find myself looking forward to the adventure of the unknown. I know a lifetime is short (and that, God forbid, my life could end tomorrow) but yet the future seems stretched out ahead and the uncertainty, while frightening at times, is exciting too. (I guess that's my weak attempt at philosophical musing, but I trust you know what I mean.)

I met Wendy on Thursday. She's doing hairdressing in Piltown with Olga Prendergast. She's got her hair permed and looks very suave. She said she'd write to you.

I heard the Goof is gone nuts on a 'Buy Irish' campaign above. It's a craze that's taken over in many schools. Also, she is now in charge of the book-borrowing scheme since 007* is in hospital. (I wonder have the KGB done something to the latter.)

---

* Sister Patrick, the retired teacher who ran the second-hand-book borrowing scheme. Neither of us could afford all new books so once we got our book list every year we went along to Sister Patrick to see if she had any of those we needed. Every year you had to answer all of her questions as to why exactly you couldn't afford new books and assure her that you had tried to get them second-hand elsewhere. She had a relatively small stock of books so she was trying to ensure they went to the most deserving. She used to wear her glasses down on her nose and would peer at you over them for what seemed like an eternity before giving you a book. We always said that any intelligence service would be proud of her interrogation techniques and nicknamed her 007.

I never find myself in
tion like that again. Rem
nter's Tale'. I heard it
I got all reminiscent,
your crush and the la
me. Isn't it great Cathy
ce we are (agewise) I m
eally enjoy being 18 cos
a degree of independence
you can act the gom if you
we're not 'all growed up'
thout sounding corny, I
yself looking forward to
venture of the unknown. I
lifetime is short (and tha
rbid, my life could end tom
nt yet the future seems
nt ahead and the uncertai
hile brightening at times, is
(I guess that's my wea

Hang on. I'm going to take a break and watch telly. (*Murphy's Micro Quiz-M* is on. It's very good. I'll be back in a minute – or half-hour!)

Hello again. Now for a bit of gossip. Guess who got engaged. Your breadman! Who knows? It might be contagious, huh! As for Mrs Denny, I'm not sure if she is or isn't. Actually, she was at the same Mass as Maw last week. Maw says she doesn't look as if she is. Poor Denny, imagine having everyone scrutinising you for tell-tale signs. I heard people asked her in school but she didn't reply. Another case for Sherlock Holmes (or even my maw)!

Actually I've seen a few of the James Bond movies. The stunts are great but without being a prude I must say all the female stars are employed for body rather than mental ability!

Anyway *Glenroe* has just started and I shamelessly admit I'm hooked. If you want a rundown I'll oblige. If not just say the word.

Finally ('Thank God,' sez you, and I don't blame you), are you or aren't you . . . coming home for Christmas? Write immediately and tell me.

Lots of love and best of luck,
Mary

PS Advice from Aunty Katie, please – how can I prevent myself from becoming a heartless, calculating capitalist and still succeed as an accountant?!

PPS My grant finally came through. I can now pay off my debts and go on a tear.

Part 2

Celebration

Winter 1983–4

Trégunc

Saturday, 3 December 1983

Dear Mary,

Thanks a million for your letter. It was so long in coming that I was beginning to think I'd said something insulting in my last reply. But it turns out that it was my fault. Over here, y'see, they're very sticky about stamps and the last time I wrote to you I hadn't put enough blinking stamps on the envelope. So, a week after I posted it, the postman hands me a letter and I says to myself, 'Janey, I knew myself and Mary wrote alike, but I didn't realise how much alike. And didn't she reply quickly too!' And then I cops on that the postman is giving me funny looks, and is waiting for the extra stamps to be added.

Also a lot of letters that I receive are somewhat short on stamps – or so they say here. I think it's all a sham to make up money! My tennis racket arrived last week. It cost Nanny £5.50 to send it (gasp!) and I'd to pay another £1.30.

Well, anyway, the six of us were at lunch when the postman came today. On Saturdays he's early and comes at eleven thirty-ish. Well, I was delighted when I got the package and knew it was from you. I absolutely massacred the envelope! I passed the photo all around the table (it's covered in sauce and grease and fish and pâté now . . . just joking!) with proud cries of 'That's Carrick, that's Carrick!' And then came 'There's my neighbours', etc. The bloody ignorant eejits thought the photo was a recent one and that it was snowing there at the moment. What kind of geography do they do here anyway?

And then Bruno who knows some English sees the name

'Catherine Cunningham' in the RIP section [of the *Opinion*] and wanted to know if that was me! Y'see, none of 'em can pronounce my name. Viv always says Coulon. I think it's because she doesn't know the difference between *u* and *n*!

Must tell ya a good one – as my grandma'd say. Had a package during the week with unfamiliar writing on it. 'Now, who's this?' I asks myself. Well, it turns out to be a book from Denny. I was thrilled to bits. Maeve Binchy's *Light a Penny Candle*. Remember we always said she was the only really human one in Greenhill (Mrs Denny that is, not Maeve Binchy!) besides the students, of course. The book was a brand new copy – never read by anyone – and it cost £2.50 to send it! I feel quite guilty. Well, I'll bring it home at Xmas, and if you don't read it, I'll bloody well do I don't know what to you! Okay? It's terrific! I laughed my heart out, bawled my eyes out and thoroughly enjoyed it. I read the six hundred pages in twenty-four hours! Good thing Viv used to be a book worm and understands.

Naturally she included a letter too. She seems in great form although the hubby's not in the best of health. She's taking Cordon Bleu classes in Clonmel. Well, the funny thing is she told me that the rumour (which had never reached my ears!) that Miss Harte was pregnant wasn't true. I nearly fell off the bed laughing when I read that. I took my courage in my two hands and told her how ironical she had been when I wrote back!

Have got very few letters lately. Wrote to Celia over a month ago and haven't heard a word since. The same applies to Eleanor. I'm getting afraid now that I said something I shouldn't have to them. Had a letter from Catherine

Cummins the same day that Denny's arrived. Y'know, I never ever read any of Catherine's English lessons the whole time I was at school. I really regret it now. Remember how intelligent and deep-thinking and Hawkeye-ish (*M*A*S*H*) we used to think she was. Boy, did we understate it! I think if I were as concerned about the problems of the world as she is, I'd jump off the bell-tower in St Phil's Church, that's if they ever finish putting the bloody thing up!

Speaking of WRTC, have you cheered up down there? Glad you got your grant. Your classmates sound terrific. Few words of advice. We all get down and out now 'n' again. Put on a weepy record and bawl for half an hour or put on a cheery one and dance for half an hour. Either way you'll feel better afterwards! At least, that works for me. Only at the moment the tape-recorder has disappeared and I can't play the record-player as it's in the same room as the telly, which goes day and night!

Have you made any friends down there? I don't mean acquaintances. What's the boy–girl relationship like? Is everyone stiff and shy, or the opposite with the type of jokes and comments you wouldn't tell your mother? D'you meet a lot of the girls from school?

Isn't it horrible asking a question and having to wait a fortnight for the reply? I said that to Sue last time I wrote. I'm really looking forward to seeing you when I come home. Be prepared to sit in Galvin's/Central Grill/ice-cream parlour or all three for at least four hours, while we catch up on all the news. I mean, it's not the same when we write, is it? D'you think we'll have changed in our reactions towards each other? I'd hate it if we had.

Was I curt in my last letter insinuating I didn't want to

hear from you when you're depressed? Please accept my apologies if I was. If telling me your problems and miseries makes you feel cheerful (and me miserable, you sadist!), please tell them to me. Think of me as your psycho-whatever it is. Enough aimless wandering!

Great news, I've got over my allergy to God's most beautiful creatures – cats. It was awful when I first arrived. If I just looked at Mimique it was sneeze, sneeze, sneeze. Now I'm sitting on my bed, while he's keeping me little tootsies warm. D'you think if I locked myself up in a glasshouse for a month I'd have no more problems with pollen?

Gerard would make a terrific psycho-whatever it is! I think most people think of me as being the fearless white warrior, afraid of nothing, overflowing with self-confidence and courage, always daring, never shy! I'm not a bit like that really. The reason I always wear rather long skirts (apart from the fact that me legs look like stumps of trees!) is so that nobody'll see my knees knocking! And I'm not exaggerating. I generally have to force myself to do things. And as for going into the big bad world all on my little ownio, well, I'd rather face that than the next fifty years in Glen! So, I think it's wrong to take people at face value and say, 'Oh, she's never afraid and is full of self-confidence etc.' End of lecture!

Speaking of Gerard, pity he's Sue's brother. I mean, if you were ever 'going' with him and broke it off afterwards, well, things would be rather difficult. I'm sure you know what I mean. Anyway, I think I'd rather have Gerard as a friend without any romantic ties. And truthfully, I can't envision any of the latter between any of us and him. I mean, can you just switch from friend to boyfriend? Vice versa, perhaps.

Can you see what I'm driving at? If not, bring it up again and I'll try to explain.

I've a feeling yourself and Sue don't spend hours on the phone each week, so hopefully all of my confidences are reasonably safe.

I'm looking forward to Sue's party even though as of yet I don't know if it's definite. Last time she wrote she said Michael was still unattached. I'm keeping my fingers crossed. But then I suppose attachments don't mean anything to him! I really intend enjoying myself this Christmas.

Last year was great – even if I felt so embarrassed about Tom. But still, the over-the-moon feeling was great while it lasted. I wonder what he thought of it all (I'm sure he was up to date)? But, then, with his fantastic looks, he's probably well used to it!

I don't know if I agree with you about it being great being eighteen. I'm kinda apprehensive, waiting for 'it all' to come. I think twenty-two, twenty-three'd be better. Then you'd be sophisticated and knowledgeable and wouldn't understand the words 'shy' and 'blush'. But when I was fifteen or sixteen I used to think you'd be as previously mentioned at the age of eighteen. I think Janis Ian's song 'At 17' could be called 'At 18' as well. But hopefully not 'At 19'!

D'you remember how worried I was (yes, I DO worry!) back in May and June and July about coming here? I was so sure I'd be a real let-down to everyone after Lena. Well, it's not a bit like that. She asked Viv if she could come back next summer but Viv wants me to stay on. She smoked non-stop. Stayed out 'til 4 a.m., got up at twelve in the day, etc., etc., etc. I really had to laugh when Viv said she was afraid of the

achel. I'm keeping my fing
ose attachments don't mea
really intend enjoying

last year was great – e
rressed about Tom. But
was great while it las
ght of it all. (I'm su
ther with his fantastic
to it!!!

I don't know if I agree wi
being 18. I'm kinda a
all" to come. I think I
be sophisticated o knowl
stand the words "sly" o "
as 15 or 16 I used
ously mentioned at the
re Jan's song" at 17" c
self. But hopefully not

D'you remember how woo
as back in May o June

way I'd turn out. You never think of the family being worried, do you? I mean, all of the sympathies lie with the au-pair.

Bruno said today that the people in the bakery next door were saying that I was better than Lena. But I think that's because being of an older generation they don't hold with people wearing shorts etc. during the summer. If I have to have a clamp fitted, I'm going to fit into a size twelve this summer!

I really intend making up for all of the nights I spent inside watching telly, reading, knitting, sewing, etc., when the summer arrives. I'm going to have a fling (please, please!). They all have the impression I think that I'm an old granny of a one, but roll on the peak season and all the young people and they'll find out. I believe that young people all over France claim relations here for the summer, and consequently end up pitching tents in their granny's cousin's sister-in-law's back garden for two or three months. I believe that there are barbecues and everything here then. But that's all six or seven months away yet!

Who's Annique? Well, she's the teacher at École Maternelle, St Phil. She's thirtyish and last week thought and was hoping she was pregnant but unfortunately it was a false alarm. She's Anne's mother and is thin and rather plain and can't really put people at their ease. Just the same I like her a lot. She's terrific with the kids.

What's this I hear about my ex-breadman being engaged? I thought he was waiting for me! And sure and all didn't I get the ring in the barm brack last year!

Will there be a Macra party this Christmas? Remember the one last year? I haven't heard 'A Winter's Tale' since that time. Sue made up a tape for me with piles of terrific songs but to my surprise and disappointment that wasn't included. Have you got any contacts in Macra now, apart from John trying to do away with you (heart failure) by saluting you?

Talking of dishy guys . . . Remember I mentioned Chantal and Yvan before? Well, due to the fact I've been keeping my ears cocked, I've come to the impression that he is divorced, looks after his son on Wednesday afternoons and is living with Chantal. Shucks! The only good-looking guy in sight. Well, not strictly true. Bruno is rather dishy too and very friendly, tall and blond, rather reminds you of a member of the Aryans (new pop group, or someone born between 23 March and 22 April!). And then, of course, there's the hunk who works in the pub a mile up the road. I've seen him three times and can't figure out if he's a Tom type, nice to everybody, a Michael (drool) type, nice to the girls, or if he's interested. But as I'm going to give up sweets for the New Year – not to mention the booze – I'll hardly find out.

Well, as it's 6.20 p.m. I'm going to doll myself up a bit, i.e. put on me jumper with only two holes, and go down for supper. See you later, I hope!

Sunday, 4 December

Last night after dinner I was too lazy to finish writing. Consequently, having had a row with Chrystelle, at the end of which I declared she could bloody well learn English herself, I find myself with an extra hour or two.

Vivianne is after me to give English lessons to adults. She's already asked the mayoress, and there'd be no problem borrowing the school hall one or two nights a week. I'm not too eager myself, though. I can't imagine myself standing up in front of a class of people, all older than me, especially with my bad French, and trying to teach them English. I think my face'd be the same colour as telephone boxes in England, permanently. I wouldn't even know where to start. I'd rather have two or three extra people and give lessons privately.

At the moment I've got two young pupils. Alain is terribly shy and it was only yesterday after eight weeks of lessons that he independently posed a question! And, what's more, actually laughed. Don't get the wrong idea that I'm scaring him – as if I'd do a thing like that! His mother always says that he says I'm 'très gentille'. Unfortunately, as he's a very good friend of the family, I don't charge him anything! Any accountant's tips on how ole Scrooge here could extract a few francs from him?!

I may have mentioned that the postman wanted me to give Véronique, his daughter, grinds. She's terribly nice – 13½ but you'd think sixteen/seventeen. She's the image of Ber Cooney. The whole family are lovely – well, there are only four of them. Véronique, her parents (both fifty-ish) and an orphaned cousin. It's rather complicated and I don't like to ask questions. You should see him – I wish I could – his photos are gorgeous, especially when he wears his army uniform. He's now living with his girlfriend and their child in Alsace or somewhere. I believe all the girls in Trégunc were after him and I'm not surprised.

Imagine, four weeks from today'll be Christmas Day! Yippee! I'm really happy to be coming home, even though it's only for a week. I've no details as to dates and travel arrangements yet. We phoned up the airport and it'd cost £200 from Lorient via Paris and London to Cork – exactly two months' wages! The boat'd work out at about £50, but from what we can work out from the timetable, it doesn't operate for the months of Jan and Feb. So, please keep your fingers crossed for me. Wouldn't it be awful if I couldn't come because of a blinking timetable?

Well, anyway, I know Christmas is only three weeks away, but I've worked out (with my computer brain!) that you'll have time to write back. Please do so, if you can manage it, as I love getting your letters. But I suppose you'll have exams coming up. Good luck in them. Keep your chin up in WRTC and make the best of all the gorgeous hunks down there!

From your
Ever-loving
Ever-devoted
Ever-amiable
Ever-kind, generous, gentille etc. etc. etc.
Me!!!!!!!!!!!!!!!

PS Hope that in all the redecorating your mother didn't throw out me coffee-table. Haven't had a decent cup of coffee since I came here (we drink from bowls or 'egg-cups'). Say 'hello' to all your family for me, and tell 'em to batten the hatches for my arrival.

Carrick

Sunday, 8 January 1984

Dear Cathy,

Have <u>you</u> survived the turkey and ham or are you like me, thanking my lucky stars that I only make a pig out of myself just once a year (well, almost just once a year)? I was really, really delighted to hear your voice gabbling down the phone. Kitty chicken, ya never sounded better.

You should have been here the morning I phoned you (God, that sounds stupid, I know, I know). I was going to phone you from Paddy Landers but then Maw decided that we'd phone from the pay phone outside the Friary. Off we went and I got through to yer wan in the exchange. She said I couldn't phone from there as there was money stuck in the slot but she told me how much it would cost. So we got the money ready and off we went to O'Donnell's (near the Old Bridge). The two of us squashed into the booth (which we shared with a stepladder!). Then Maw wanted to be on the side where the slot is to put in the money so we had to do a little shuffle (or hucklebuck!). When yer wan finally got the number and asked us to put in the money some of it fell on the floor and Maw got a cramp while bending down to pick it up. Then the telephone started choking and spitting out the money, which we promptly replaced, but yer wan wouldn't put me through 'cos she said I hadn't put the money in. Maw pushed open the door and hollered for Michael O'Donnell, who came and assured yer wan that we <u>had</u> paid. Honestly, the things I do for you!

Here's the Treasure Hunt. I've put some of the answers on the back of the page. See can you guess before you look at em.

CARRICK-ON-SUIR MACRA NA FEIRME TREASURE HUNT.

Q. = QUESTION,   D. = DIRECTION,   L. = LEFT,   R. = RIGHT

Start at Garda Barracks Barracks between 1.45 p.m. e   3.00 p.m.

Finish at Tony Kehoe's by 4.30 p.m.

Route - up New Street, over New Bridge, turn right straight through next two crossroads on to Coolnamuck Road, up to Kilsheelan and down the Main Road.

All questions can be answered without getting out of your cars.

Put your answers on sheet provided.

D.   As you approach the Timber Yard from the side.

Q.1. What does the Arch have to say for itself?

D.   On to Main Road soon

Q.2. Mix this and it will make the washing easier.

D.   Drive on past the houses on right.

Q.3 .You can only go through, if you've got only TWO.

D.   On a small bit.

Q.4. What can you almost double from here?

D.   On past last house on right.

Q.5. What mobilises "Rick"?

D.   On another small bit.

Q.6.. What former President (Close to your hearts) might you find here?

D.   Another small bit.

Q.7 Why does this pier, give no cheer, to those around here?

D.   On past the red gate.

Q.8. What rises here is very clear.

D.   On to stud farm.

Q.9 How many on this Swan Team?

D.   Drive on past Rathgormack junction and Castle.

Q10. If these were to fall, what would you call?

D.   On a bit now past the farmhouse on right.

Q.11. If the first you do not see, look at the rest and an owl there may be.

D.   On another bit, near the bends.

Q.12. A piercing object, in mourning perhaps.

D.   Just around the turns.

Q.13. What is doubly "stylish"?

D.   On past "Beware of Bull" sign.

Q.14.Find the decade surrounding the L.P. OK?

D.   On a small bit.

To crown it all, when we got home we were locked out ('cos Maw lost the key) and after fifteen minutes (slight exaggeration, perhaps) of yelling and roaring like lunatics while bashing on the door knocker we finally persuaded Da, who was resurrected from his hibernation, to throw us down his key. I dread to think what the new neighbours think of us! They're a young couple with two kids; he is Tony Dunne's stepbrother. And believe it or not I haven't seen them properly yet (as peeking thru the curtains doesn't count), let alone spoken to 'em.

I really enjoyed Christmas but I can't tell you how disappointed I was that you didn't come.* I went to the Macra party in Ballyneale on the Friday before Christmas Eve. There was a car treasure hunt beforehand. Sue came a-calling and we walked to the Guards Barracks where we were joined by Anne Cummins and Dolly. Ann Delaney gave us a lift on the treasure hunt. Gerard, Pat and John Foley, Godfrey Green and Co were in another car and we had great gas dodging each other on the road out. At one stage we parked the car and bent down low inside. When they passed they thought we were gone into the field (it was pitch dark, remember). So they doubled back. Such laughing. Then they parked in front of one of the clues and wouldn't budge. We passed them out and slowed down to 5 m.p.h. so they couldn't pass.

The party itself, like all Macra dos, took <u>ages</u> to get off the ground. Just picture it – us girls sitting around by the wall while all the fellas stood in the middle discussing scour, hoose and Ranezol! (Honest!) I danced nearly all the dances with Gerard. It

* Catherine was not able to get home to Carrick for Christmas and spent it with her father and sister Celia in London.

was awkward because I couldn't dance with anyone else then, because he kept asking me. To tell you the truth, I've gone right off him. Oh, he's okay and very friendly but somehow I think he tries too hard or something. I can't place my finger on it but he seems different. What he said sort of sounded false or something. Maybe he used too many clichés, I dunno . . .

I enjoyed Sue's party more. I think it's because all the lads* were there. Eleanor looked great. Did you know she has to wear a veil?[†] Yeah, and she's leaving her hair grow so that she can tie it up. She was in great spirits. Anne and Mary Maher were there too. Mary is teacher-training. I had a great chat with Catherine. I think she's regretting not doing science 'cos I said, 'Do you feel there's something missing with your accountancy course?' And she said, 'Yeah! Physics, chemistry and biology.' Ber was in great glee. Kathleen looked absolutely stunning but was really shy. At one stage Michael (heartthrob) was trying hard to impress (you know the sort of thing!) but she was real shy and didn't answer him so he just gave up. I can see what you mean – he really is something! The only damper was that Tom wasn't there. Oh, I nearly forgot: K— got off with R— at the Macra party and was with her at Sue's too. He drove her home – with me and Eleanor in the back! Did you ever wish you could disappear? He turned off the lights when he got to her place and got out with her around the back of the car, leaving Eleanor and me twiddling our thumbs! Got home at 2.15 a.m. (an improvement on the Macra party, which was twenty to four!).

* Girls.
† Eleanor was training to be a nurse in Dr Steevens' Hospital in Dublin. It was one of the last hospitals that insisted that the trainee nurses wear full veils (just like novices in a convent). Even in 1983 that was unusual.

Q1 Answer: Carrick Beg House (written on the Arch)

Q4 Answer: The Speed

Q5 Answer: Car. (Signpost says "Carrick on Suir")

Q6 Answer: Paddy Lane (we passed a laneway)

Q7 Answer: Tar the farmers was written on it

Q9 Answer: This was very hard. The answer was the number of fence posts at O'Gorman's. They were painted Black & White (the colours of the Swan)

Q10 Answer: Timber (there were trees past Wendy's house)

Q11 We got this one wrong. We thought it might be a barn but actually there was a sign saying 'NO SHOOTING'. If you didn't see the S then it would be "No Hooting"

Q12 This was a road sign.

Q13 You know that graveyard down past Smith's. Well there's two styles going into it.

Q14 LP was written on the ground and the numbers round it added up to 10.

Q15 We were looking for this for ages. We thought it might be Smith's goat !!! (Such laughin' we had) Actually you know that Bridge below Smith's, if you take away the g you have Bride. It is white as snow etc.
THE ROSMINIANS

Q16 We parked outside your gate for these. The first one we got wrong. The answer was 'mini' in the middle of Rosminians — on the name plate.

I met Sue's digs mate, Caroline, at the party. She's really, really nice (just like us – modest as well!). Actually when she was dancing her resemblance to you was uncanny. Many people remarked on it.

You should have seen us all gathered in Sue's sitting room around the phone – six girls and Michael. He told Sue's father to close the door and give him privacy. He looked lovely sitting on the floor talking to you!

U— lost her baby. It was really sad. She went into labour on Sunday night and they left her until Tuesday night before doing a Caesarean section. The child died only an hour before the section was done. So really it was pure neglect. U— is heart-broken. Talking about child fatalities, there have been a lot of child deaths in Carrick in the past two months. And every single birth I've heard of in the past few months has been a Caesarean section. Is it that we're all getting weak, or what?

I meant to ask you, did you bring out the tape-recorder with you and did Viv teach you any crafts and are there more young people in Trégunc and did you unearth why the staff have only been there six months and . . .?

Some more gossip – did you know that Cheryl is going to Canada as an au-pair for two years? I met her sister yesterday and she told me. That's all the details I have for now, though. Did you know that Finola is now going out with Donogh (across the road from moi)? Apparently it all arose from the pantomime (which they were both in)! Guess who's joining the panto next year?!

I bet you're disappointed that Denny isn't. So am I. Guess it's the ould maternal instinct (huh).

Next time you come home (that's if you ever do come home), there'll be a new restaurant. I think it's Chinese but I'm not sure so you'd better get crackin' with your chopsticks!!

I went to the sales yesterday. Susan Kelly is working in Tom Whelan's shoe shop now. I bought a pair of Puma trainers (£11.95).

You know the way my aunt Joan smokes like a trooper. Well, she went to this hypnotist guy in Dungarvan and, guess what, she gave up the weed. I couldn't believe it 'cos she couldn't stay off them for an hour. She's lasted three weeks but I met her yesterday and she says she's going back on them again. One thing, though – she's gone real absent-minded and giggly. She almost didn't see me yesterday (and me straight in front of her) and that's definitely NOT like Joan who is usually razor sharp. I wonder if it's anything to do with the hypnosis. Kind of scary really, isn't it?

Maw, Paw and Matty are fine. One day Maw asked me if I'd have tea. I said I'd go get a Coke instead. I poured it out, turned my back and when I turned around again she'd poured milk into my Coke. Honest!

We won a Christmas cake in Farrells' draw. We also went for a walk up Pill Road on St Stephen's Day. You wouldn't recognise it. You can see the bungalow from the road now (the one beside the school) and the wall in front of the school is continued all the way down to the terraced houses. It makes the road feel really <u>long</u>.

Guess what? I failed my first exam <u>ever</u> before Christmas. It was Statistics. It was really funny. I wasn't too disappointed as Niamh got exactly the same mark (phew!). We got 43 (50 is a pass). Harry got 94 and Marita* got 10 so . . .

I've watched a lot of TV over the holliers. I'm sorry that I can't tell you what's happening in *Dynasty*. If you want to know about *Dallas* or *Glenroe* I'd be more than happy to fill you in!

I'm going back to college tomorrow. I'm really looking forward

* Marita joined the class a few weeks in.

to it. I love the atmosphere down there. There's a kind of solidarity you feel being with others your own age. So, Kitty girl, I'd better go now or I'll run out of paper, words, gossip and immaculate writing! Hope you like the calendar. I've sent a photo taken last Christmas too in Anne-Marie's.

Byeeeeee.
Lots of love.
Write soon.
Mary

Trégunc

Thursday, 19 January 1984

Dear Mary,

Thanks a million for your letter, which was impatiently received after all these long weeks of waiting. As both Chantal and Yvan have Thursday off, I sometimes give a hand in the restaurant, emptying the dishwasher and the like. So there I was up to me elbows in soup and rice and pork and pâté and apple tart and pineapple and kirsch, and I'll leave the other gory details to yourself, when the letter arrived. Now, of course, being the conscientious worker I am I didn't like to take time off to read it, so it was about an hour later I finally got to open the envelope! I'm sure you can imagine the state I was in by that stage.

So anyway, at about two o'clock, I took myself up to the bedroom, put on *Best Moves* by Chris de Burgh (which finally arrived from home!), stretched out on the bed, with Mimique on my knees, and spent a very pleasant half an hour exploring the glories from the West! I just ADORE the calendar, photo is lovely too, but best of all is the letter! I love getting the type of letter you write, with all the little bits of gossip and snippets of useless, irrelevant info. When they write to me from Glen, they tell me nothing at all, which is most annoying!

Now, where do I start? As I've already gone into detail about my holiday in London to Sue and Catherine, I don't think I'll start there. Well, at any rate, I won't blab on about the shopping, Oxford St, Hammersmith, cooking, washing up, etc. But, in a way I was very disappointed; not with the holiday itself or anything. After being stuck out here miles from family and friends for so long, I was really looking forward to seeing Celia again and being able to have some nice long chats, y'know, girl to girl. But, boy, was I doomed to failure! I'm not sure how to explain. But she didn't seem in the least bit interested. During the ten days I was there, she never asked ONE single question. I mean, it's been seven months since we met, and nothing! Just as I was beginning to think we were getting closer. But any time we were alone she just watched television. She didn't seem to want to talk at all.

When I mentioned anything about France she acted bored, so after the first few days I gave up. Even when I mentioned things that happened during the summer, she didn't want to know. As for info about her college, ever try getting blood out of a turnip? I think if I'd stayed there much longer, we'd have ended up having a row! Even Daddy didn't put himself out in that field. Even though I'm still his favourite (what modesty!) I kinda got the impression he wasn't particularly interested. Funnily enough it was Maura* who asked the most. Yes, we did meet! As a matter of fact, Celia and I had her up to dinner one night. Naturally with us cooking, the meal wasn't fantastic. But there weren't any awkward silences! We weren't exactly chummy with each other, merely polite. We went out together on New Year's Eve. Michael, her second son, came too. It's been eight or nine years since I've seen him. Boy, what a change! He ALWAYS wears black, has dark hair, dark eyes, is a bit taller

---

* Catherine's father's partner.

than me, and only his lack of years and money prevents him from being the perfect Mills & Boon hero! Both of these faults, however, can be rectified! By the way, he's a government-employed artist!

Okay, end of that boring subject. I expect that by this stage M— has had her baby. What was it? I feel very sorry for her married with a family at her age! Mind you, I intend being in that position myself in about ten years! Who's opened the new restaurant in Carrick? Where? Why? When? I've beaten you to it with the chopsticks – more about that later! If you see the Smiths, tell them I was asking for them.

I'd have given anything to have seen yourself and your maw in the phone box the day you phoned! I see some things never change: the P&T, that is! But I'd have given even more to have seen you all at Sue's party. It was nice talking to you all on the phone, though. I felt very homesick afterwards. Please, please, pass on any snippets you can think of concerning the party. Y'know, I didn't feel in the least bit over the moon when I was talking to Michael. But the next night at Hammersmith (ask Sue) I spent the whole time thinking about him, and none of the other guys there were a patch on him! Were you talking to him? Did he say anything after the call? I get the impression that you can finally see what it is all the other girls see in him. There really is something about him, isn't there? I suppose he's kinda unforgettable!

Terribly sorry about U—'s baby. You know, it doesn't seem so long ago that you were telling me she was pregnant. Where does the time go? When I brought Thomas to school today there were some kids playing in the yard. Do you remember the noise they make? I do. I felt like crying. A short time ago, I was part of that noise. And now I'm on the other side of the fence. It makes me feel old!

Remember me saying that I used to teach the kids English? Well, I went to the school one day, and Annique came over to me and said that I couldn't do that any more. A small minority of the parents were against it. They felt that their children had enough problems with their native language, never mind learning a foreign one! Annique was terribly embarrassed – y'see, it was she who asked me to do it in the first place. So now I just leave Thomas off at the door. But whenever the kids see me, they come running over for a kiss, which is a great boost for the morale! I'd love to make a video of it and send it to Lena! That'd make her swallow her bitchy sarcastic remarks!

I couldn't figure out for ages why Chrystelle didn't like me. I know I'm not in the Eleanor league as far as being pleasant is concerned, but just the same, apart from giving her a well-deserved belt now and again, I'm generally quite pleasant, aren't I? Well, anyway, I suddenly copped on the other day in the course of conversation. She's jealous because I get on so well with Thomas. Y'see, she's crazy about him herself. The other day she was complaining because there was a tiny wrinkle in her sweatshirt which I'd ironed, so Viv told her she could go and iron it herself the next time!

Gerard – it's funny that you should say he appeared different somehow to you. I always found him very natural. False is a word I'd never associate with him. Perhaps you're seeing too much of him. I don't mean that in a romantic way, incidentally! But I know what you mean when you say nobody else got to dance with you because of him. It can be annoying, can't it? Was Tom at the Macra party? I remember last year I did the drying up with him – how romantic! Sue said that Ger had asked Eleanor to the Macra social. You never mentioned it, didn't you know about it? Or is it that you just think it's a once-off thing? I remember the night we went to Kats, they were together the whole time. If you know anything be sure and pass it along, won't you?

Sue said she had the impression you were all rather shocked at her behaviour at the party. She seems to be trying to live her whole life at once. From her letters I can see that she's really making the most of things in the NIHE. I suppose she's right in a way. I fully intend having a good time once the summer arrives. As of yet I've met nobody my own age. So, roll on, peak season, and I'll make up for all of that! How are relationships going in WRTC? Have you made any friends? I don't mean acquaintances!

Remember the photos taken at the last party? Well, I forgot to bring them to France with me. I left them at home in one of my drawers. Now I'm terrified that Nanny will find them. And even though the only thing blue in them is my dress, well, you know what grandmothers are like – especially mine! By the way every single time she writes, she asks me to come home and get a job in Ireland. And I thought she'd be glad to see the back of me! And Granddad, whom I've seen only two or three times writing letters, always writes to me! People are surprising, aren't they?

At the moment I'm ploughing through a Harold Robbins novel. Y'know, I'm glad I'm not rich. They seem to spend all their time bed-hopping, wife-swapping, getting married and divorced, and being generally miserable and unhappy. It's very depressing really. A bit like *Light a Penny Candle* even though there's no other resemblance between them!

Right now, I'm supposed to be doing my next lesson in typing, but I keep making piles of mistakes, so I've given it up until I'm in a better humour for it! As you can see, I haven't changed a bit! Would you like an example of what I'm supposed to do?

âtre pâtre plâtre idolâtre mulâtre albâtre être fenêtre pôle pâle être pâtre plâtre idolâtre

I type the line five times, and then I do likewise for the other ten or so. Every week, I send away a lesson, which is corrected. The course is very expensive; about £30 a month. I get paid £100, but due to my recent holidays and financial problems for the LeClercqs, I'm currently skint! I put a notice in a few shop windows yesterday, which read as follows:

> *Mlle CONLON (Anglaise) donnerait des cours d'anglais*
> *aux élèves au 6ème à la terminale.*
> *Tous les jours (30F l'heure)*
> *S'adresser . . .*

Hopefully I should get a few replies soon. I've worked out that three people a week would pay for my correspondence. I know the course is terribly expensive, but if I were to do it in WRTC wouldn't it work out much dearer? At least here I make about seventy quid a month. Also I'm more independent here.

I'm delighted to hear about the Carrick-made tape. I have a tape-recorder at my disposal, so I'd be delighted if you could manage to make a recording of the tape for me. What's Shirley Carson doing now?

Ah, yes, chopsticks! It was François's birthday on 7 Jan so there was a little bit of a party here, just the people in the restaurant and me. The kids were packed off to bed – for once – so it was a great night. Over here, I'm terribly shy, and never open my mouth at meals, except when just the family are there. But the night of the party, everybody was terribly nice. I sat beside Yvan, who looked even more gorgeous than usual and FLIRTED with me! A great morale booster, even though none of us was serious! I think I was the teeniest, weeniest bit tipsy. Anyway, it was a brilliant night, and I really enjoyed myself. It finished at about three in the morning, after the coffee and the champagne. Nearly forgot, the food was KOREAN! It was out of this world. Absolutely fantastic! Now I know why the war lasted so long there! And I didn't make a fool of myself with the chopsticks. As a matter of fact, it was Chantal who finally gave up and used a spoon.

U asked me about handcrafts. At the moment, I'm halfway thru my second tapestry. It's about a foot square and is of a dog. The other one was of a Breton church. Viv and I framed it ourselves and I sent it to Nanny and Granddad for Christmas, as well as a nightdress each for the twins, which I also made. I got a letter from home last week, and there wasn't a single mention of the parcel. I was terribly hurt, until common sense prevailed, and I realised that it probably hadn't arrived. I hope it's not lost in the post.

I think that by this stage I'm running out of news. Oh, Viv and François are trying to buy the restaurant from Viv's mother. Hence, it's nothing but meetings with bank managers and the like now. Anyway, they are getting fairly browned off with the whole thing. So, she says to me last week, 'How'd u like to go to America?!' (only she said it in French!) It turns out that Yvan has a brother there. So, he's going to find out all the details, and if things work out badly with the banks, they're thinking of moving lock, stock and barrel to the States. In other words, the family, cat, dog, staff, me and French cuisine. But I know Viv by this stage – the whole plan will be forgotten!

Not exactly enthusiastic about *Dallas* or *Glenroe*, but at the same time must admit that I wouldn't be averse to hearing what's happening! And why the hell can't u tell me about *Dynasty*? Huh?! You'd better have a good excuse, mate!

In the course of her investigations amongst my stuff last night, Delphine came across the photo u sent of yourself. They all said we looked alike. I remember a lot of people used to think we were sisters. I'd love to have u as a sister!

And on that note, I'm going to close the typewriter, and head to the piano for a half-hour's practice. I'm progressing slowly in that field, as in all others! I beg your forgiveness for the quality of my typing. I should have improved somewhat the next time I write.

PLEASE WRITE BACK VERY SOON OR ELSE . . . (I'll cry!)
Kilograms and kilograms of love,
Catherine

Be sure and say hello to all the family for me. I know it's a bit late but all the same, HAPPY NEW YEAR!

PS By the way, when I wrote back to Denny, I mentioned I'd heard she was pregnant (but didn't give her any informers' names). She sent a Christmas card to Glen as I'd told her I was coming home. She asked me to try to drop in and see her. Now I don't know if I should write back to her or wait for a letter. I haven't heard from Reggie for ages. If you have any school gossip, please pass it on to me. All the twins talk about are the new students* next door!

PPS Are you keeping in touch with Sue? Towards the end of the summer I kinda got the impression you'd really lost contact. That's partly why I don't tell the two of you the same things in my letters. If I tell you half the news, and her the other half, hopefully you'll telephone each other to catch up!

* Student priests and brothers. Catherine's home was next door to the Rosminian order's college at Glencomeragh.

Carrick

Sunday, 5 February 1984

Dearest Cathy,

A thousand apologies for the delay in writing. 'The fault, dear
Cathy, is not in our stars but in ourselves that we are lazy'!
Seriously, though, I just didn't get around to it but any road here I
am. Actually your letter was late coming too. I came home
Monday, looked searchingly at the letter rack and my face fell. A
repeat performance on Tuesday and Wednesday. Finally on
Thursday, on seeing my face fall for the fourth time, Maw put me
out of my misery. Actually she'd hidden the letter to see my
reaction (sadist!).

Then I picked it up. Sez I, 'Wot's goin' on? It's real thin, like. Has
she fallen out with me or sommat?' Then I discovered the typing,
which I must add was really good. Now, there's one flaw, Kitty
chicken. You see, I possess a nosy maw who's particularly
interested in one Catherine Conlon who is practically part of the
family (on second thoughts forget the 'practically'). And, you see,
the only thing that prevented her from reading your writing was
– your writing! Therefore I could translate – leaving out the bits I
wanted to. In other words, I CENSORED my maw's reading. After
all, your letters are not suitable for impressionable maws, are
they?! Now, she can read them herself when you type them. Dear
Frankie, what can I do . . .?

Just to tell you how you're revered in this here homestead. As
you may or may not know, we've had <u>very</u> cold, snowy, sleety
weather here (which I've enjoyed immensely!). Anyway, one cold

and frosty morning I had to return home (actually slide home) again 'cos the omnibus didn't come because of the icy roads. When finally I convinced her to open the door to me, she settled me in front of the warm heater with a cup of steaming coffee. But d'ya think I got the coffee-table? Ya must be jokin'. Not for me the luxury of a table, oh, no. Instead she pulled over the chair! Upon questioning and interrogation she said merrily, 'Sure, that's for Catherine!'

I haven't heard from Sue in AGES ('cos the phone box is out of order). I know it's terrible hassle for you to repeat everything twice but believe me I would be ETERNALLY grateful! Actually she took me by storm at the Christmas party. Very outgoing; first out on the dance floor etc. At one stage she was precariously seated upon not one but two gentlemen. Tut, tut, what's the world coming to! Seriously, though, she really enjoyed herself and I'm glad she's so happy.

By the way (for a bit of GOSSIP or, as you put it, useless irrelevant bits and pieces!) Y— still didn't have her baby. She must have been way, way out in her dates. The restaurant hasn't opened yet and any info on it seems to have fallen off the grapevine!

Cheryl is going to Canada as an au-pair to Dr Prendeville's daughter or someone. I'm not really sure actually as I haven't spoken directly to Cheryl. When I do I'll pass on any info. I haven't had trace or tidings of Eleanor. Catherine told me all right that she went to the Macra dance with Gerard. A lovely couple, don't you think? I see Catherine very often and we have a good old natter about the times past, present and future.

I got a letter from Annette after all these months. You know

Annette's letters, though – nine sentences. It seems she's very busy, was away with the Youth Orchestra until a while ago (she didn't say where) and now is playing in the RTÉ Concert Orchestra. (I guess she means full time and professionally, but I'm not sure.) She also said she was in Paris for a week recently representing Ireland and enjoyed it. That's all she said!

Guess who's engaged – Bridget Walsh from Sir John's and Maria Walsh (not to each other, dum-dum!). By the time you come home, when the two of us re-haunt the ice-cream parlour, we'll bump into all the auld classmates pushing prams. I feel like Methuselah. To think I've never had a proper date yet.

I'm stuck into Mills & Boons again. Jackie Earl gave some to Martin for me. So this weekend I've read three Mills & Boons already. I wonder if that's a symptom of something. Remember yourself?

I'm really enjoying WRTC at the moment. I'm getting on okay with the fellas (much to my own surprise) although sometimes I'm completely ignored. Funnily enough, I like it then 'cos I get to see what they're really like without pretence. Catherine, I've just discovered something, boys do discuss girls. I've noticed it a few times sitting beside 'em in the canteen (I eavesdropped!). It came as a complete surprise. Admittedly, most of the discussion is concerned with looks, figures, etc., although not always. It's most amusing if I'm sitting in the library at a table with all fellas and a girl passes by. 'Cor,' they all say and other comments before realising I'm present and becoming contrite. I really think our segregated educ. system has a lot to answer for in relation to polarisation and ignorance of sexes. Cathy Cummins even made the same comment.

complete surprise. Familiarly ...
... of the discussion is concerned ...
looks, figures etc although no...
always. It's most amusing if ...
sitting in the library at a ta...
with all fellas and a girl p...
by 'Cox' they all say and ...
... then comments before realise...
I'm present and becoming con...
Really think our segregated
... due. system has a lot to ans...
... in relation to polarisation
and ignorance of sexes. Cat...
Cummins even made the sam...
comment.

However Cathy I'm stil...
... not happy about the course
Actually, to tell the truth I...
... now if I'm happy or not!
My emotional gears seem to b...
... neutral as far as Accountancy ...
concerned. Needless to say tha...
... not too helpful where study ...

However, Cathy, I'm still not happy about the course. Actually, to tell the truth, I don't know if I'm happy or not! My emotional gears seem to be in neutral as far as accountancy is concerned. Needless to say, that isn't too helpful where study is concerned. You really need enthusiasm. I hate leaving things slide, but what else can I do? I guess deep down I don't totally agree with all this consumerism and capitalism. Maybe I feel intimidated by the wealth and different experiences of some of my classmates. They all seem to have travelled, gone on holidays, driven cars, etc. And yet they're not intentionally snobs. I guess it's impossible to sometimes put yourself in another's position when your background and upbringing is at complete variance. I dunno . . .

Anyway, on a much more cheerful note, I think I may have glimpsed the infamous C— R— at Christmas. He was bringing in blocks next door and guess who was peering through the curtains? Unfortunately, with my eyesight (or lack of it!), I couldn't see much. Maw compares me to the guy in *F Troop* who keeps falling into the well! I really must get my glasses changed again.

Did you get any students for your English classes yet? I wish you the best of luck with it all. When are you going to Paris? I'd love to join you. (Who knows? Elephants might fly!)

By the way, remember S— O—? He's (wait for it) ENGAGED. Actually there seems to be an epidemic round here at the moment. By all accounts his maw doesn't seem too pleased and has thrown him out (no easy task – tee-hee!). The lucky woman is from Waterford. Never fear, Kitty me darlin', there's hope for us yet!

Janette is below in WRTC doing music. I've sent you the *Carrick Opinion*s covering the Miss Carrick. Did you see who they were?

Susan, Finola, etc.! Actually I was persuaded not to enter 'cos the others wouldn't have a chance and that wouldn't be fair, would it?

I met Cooney. She said the Pre-Leaving is coming up soon. They've just been filling in CAOs and applications. I sure hope that none of 'em are as unsure as I am career-wise!

Anyway, I'd better shurrup as I have a pain in me hand (no doubt you've one in your head from the scribble!). I <u>promise</u> to write sooner (honest Injun!). Maw, Paw and Matty send you the best.

Bye for now.

Lots and lots of love,
Mary

PS Write soon yerself.

PPS I was stunned, flabbergasted, etc., that you advertised yourself as Anglaise. After all poor Hally said!

Trégunc

Friday, 10 February 1984

Dear Mary,

Thanks a million for your letter, which arrived today. I think I should warn you that the one I've just started is very likely going to have to wait until next week to be posted. And I'm really sorry that you're going to have to go thru what I go thru every day, waiting for the postman, praying that he'll have a letter for me, and feeling the rest of the day put out when he hasn't! But I have a number of legitimate reasons, which I enumerate now, to put you out of your misery, and go into detail later.

1. Too much to do at the moment
2. Trip to Paris
3. Inadeptness at typing

And to go into rather more details on no. 3, I'm feeling rather pleased at myself at the moment as I've finished the first book on typing a week ahead of schedule. Book Two has mainly to do with perfecting the art, and learning how to type business doc. It's very interesting, really, and I must admit I like it. Also, I think it gives all my readers' (joke!) eyes a rest. I think my typing is more legible than my writing, which admittedly wouldn't be hard! By the way, hi, Mrs Phelan, how're you keeping?!

I think your reason for not keeping in touch with Sue is absolute rot. I recall the phone boxes in Carrick being awful, but surely you can find one in working order, somewhere in the town? Anyway, I'm going to be very mean and not tell you about the Omar Sharif look-a-like, who spent the whole night (!) pestering me, until I told him I was engaged to a cop. So, if you want to hear more about that, you'll HAVE to phone Sue.

Despite the fact that I had a dream one night that six people asked me to give them courses in English (yippee! Eighteen quid), in reality, absolutely NOBODY has done so! To tell the truth, I'm very surprised. I mean there are quite a few secondary students in the area, and the people here are absolutely rolling in money. So, please, keep your fingers crossed for me and hopefully, but doubtfully, I'll have at least one.

I'd say that you were fit to kill Annette. I hate that kind of letter, the type that tells you so much, or rather so little, and leaves you dying of suspense. Mind you, you did better than little old me who got nothing at all! I suppose the next time I hear of her will be a poster advertising a concert or something similar!

When I read of all the old classmates who have got engaged, I went up to the bathroom, had a good gawk at me mush, and counted all me grey hairs. But to tell the truth, I've absolutely NO intention of getting that serious at nineteen. But that's not saying I'd say no to heading in that direction, if the occasion just sort of happened to arise. I'm hoping that it will this summer! And cows have wings and fly!

And this ties in with your current obsession for Mills & Boons! It's an awful nuisance, isn't it? This absolute compulsion to devour them without stopping! At Christmas, I read at least fifteen of them! Without exaggerating, I read most nights until about two o'clock. I mean, between that and everything else, it's no wonder I was exhausted when I came back!

I agree with you in that our segregated school system has a lot to answer for. I think that I may have already mentioned this to Catherine, I mean, whoever came up with the idea of sticking boys in one building and girls in another must have been out of his tiny skull. I mean, it really can cause integration problems afterwards, can't it? I didn't realise boys discussed girls. Do they discuss us the way we discuss them, or is it, as you briefly mentioned, all the surface they talk about? Please pass on any related info.

Speaking of boys, in her last letter Sue said that this term she's going to settle down to study. Would you believe it she's still as stuck on M— and C— as ever. Remember, she first started on about M— in about first year, and that's one hell of a long crush. As for C—, well, she'd have better luck trying to swim to the moon, in my esteemed opinion! You've met him, haven't you? I met him a couple of times, but never saw anything in him, until the day I lost my bag in Clonmel. We went to his house, believing Gerard was there, but he wasn't. Anyway, C— turned to go into the kitchen, and I don't know if it was the light or what but he looked absolutely GORGEOUS! What would Sue do without a brother like Gerard to introduce her to all his good-looking friends?!

Since I started this letter at half one today, I've had a number of interruptions, which are, briefly, made a cup of coffee, dressed Thomas after his nap, separated the girls who were fighting, emptied the washing-machine, changed the tape (Simon and Garfunkel *Greatest Hits*) and finally brought Thomas and Delphine to the beach, where we met Annique and Anne. So, consequently, it is now almost seven in the evening. And we'll be eating in about twenty minutes, so I won't get much written now either!

If you've any eyes in your head you'll have copped on that, despite the fact it's Friday, the kids haven't any school. Mid-term break here lasts from 3 Feb to 13 Feb. And naturally until the past few days the weather was awful, which meant we couldn't go out. Thank God for the telly and video, which helped to keep them occupied, except they spent the whole time fighting over which channel to watch, which tended to get rather noisy at times, especially after I'd given the three of them a belt in the ear!

Also, as Chantal and Yvan are on two weeks' holidays at the moment, there are only three of them in the restaurant, and you need at the VERY minimum four, so I give a hand every day for an hour. I just empty the dishwasher, which isn't hard. As well as all of that, the woman who generally comes a few mornings a week didn't come this week. I don't know why. So, contrary to the normal, I've been rather busy, and will continue to be so for the next week. Hence this letter will take some time to write.

Sunday, 12 February

Celia got this great little camera at Boots just before Christmas. So, of course, she spent the whole holidays trying it out.

Anyway, the result was a fat envelope last week, containing a loan of the photos. They really turned out terrific and everyone turned out marvellously, even me! She asked me to send them back at once, but as I had a letter all ready to send to Sue, I was rather naughty, and sent four of them to her. So, if you get in touch with her immediately, you might get to see them before she sends them back to me. But can you please impress on Sue that if I don't get them reasonably soon I'm likely to be hanged, drawn and quartered!

I was supposed to go to Paris on about the seventeenth of this month. As you may know, Viv's sister was supposed to give me a loan of her apartment as she was going skiing. But it turns out she's not going on hols after all! I've been looking forward to going since it was arranged last Sept, and now, nothing. But Viv says that by hook or by crook she'll arrange something. But I'll probably end up waiting until after the season. Do you think it's some kind of plot to get me to stay on?! And as well as that, I was supposed to have a guide, a workmate of Annie's, to show me around. I don't fancy trying to find my own way around the city. He was going to take his hols the same time as me. That means, of course, that when – and if – I eventually get there, Pierre will be working. I really think I was born under an unlucky star.

I meant to ask you the last time I wrote, how's the telephone going (and don't say 'dring!') at your grandma's? Also, is Joan still off the fags? And are there still cats jumping in and out of the window in your kitchen? And is your mother keeping a shine on 'my' coffee-table? There are times when I could certainly do with a cup of her coffee – the stuff here is disgusting!! Hey, do ya think ya could buy us a flask, huh?

Thanks for the newspapers too. Was the 'Miss Carrick' fixed? I think Finola, Jackie Murphy or Susan Kelly all looked much nicer than the winner. But maybe I'm being unfair and she just doesn't take a good photo. And I suppose personality comes into it too.

Y'know, it suddenly hit me this morning (in Mass!) that I really don't know anything about your course. Well, I know what subjects you're doing and what the people in your class are like, but that's all I know. Let's be more specific. How long does the course last for? Do you go working for W & G immediately afterwards? Do you get a degree or something? What does the contract you signed say? What happens if you break it? When are you opening your own offices?! It'll be great when I'm rich and famous, having a friend who's an accountant, I mean. That way you can fiddle my books, so that I can become even richer!

Monday, 13 February

Despite the fact that Thomas can occasionally be an absolute brat, he really is a fantastic kid. He's very funny, cute and cuddly, and I'd love to have a son like him, in about ten years' time. As a matter of fact, I think that a lot of people believe he is my kid! For example, one day last week, I was in the wool shop in Trégunc, and Thomas said something. The girl behind the counter exclaimed, 'Oh, he speaks French too!' So I just kinda stared at her with me gob opened, until she said, 'He's your son, isn't he?' Then I copped on! Generally, I don't mind even if I feel that I'm far too young to have a kid that age, of any age as a matter of fact! Actually I often feel sorta proud, like yesterday, when we went for our usual Sunday afternoon walk on the beach. This couple passed, and T said hello, and gave a BEAUTIFUL smile. And the lady said that he was 'mignon'. I felt about ten feet tall!

But that works both ways. A bit later, there was this really dishy guy, walking his dog, and Thomas went over to rub the dog. I'm sure the guy thought Thomas was mine. <u>That</u> I do not like! I must make the whole thing clear when the summer and gorgeous fellas (I hope!) arrive. Otherwise, things could be rather boring and dull for me.

Had a letter from Eleanor today. She seems in fine form, but a bit upset because her weekend off had been suddenly changed. I think she's very much a home bird, and who wouldn't be with a home and family like hers? She also included two photos, one where she was smooching with a skeleton, another of herself and Ger at a social (only in that one they WEREN'T smooching, sob, sob!).

A letter from Anne arrived too. She had lovely notepaper, perhaps you've seen it? She said she was going to write to you. Speaking of paper, I adore yours! Where'd you nick it? I get the impression that the pad is really thick as you always write gorgeous long letters, and I've about five of them on the same paper. It's cute!

I'm sending you the train ticket I had at Christmas. Also enclosed is the timetable I had to follow. It was rather frightening, especially as I kept thinking of the song 'Lost In France'!

Thank God, the kids are back at school, so I'll have a bit of peace and quiet now, for a few hours every day. Gosh, that sounds like an old married matron! I've had a headache since I don't know when. But that could be partly blamed on my goggles. Now that I'm not going to Gay Paris I'll have enuf money to get them changed. I imagine it'll work out at about a month's wages, i.e. £100, which isn't too bad.

I won't finish this letter by saying, 'Well, I've run out of news now', for the simple reason I believe that I didn't give you any news!

So, I'll just shut up, with the warning that I'll throw a fit if I don't hear from you very soon.

Lots of love, and miss you all at 63,
Catherine

14 February – PS Did you get any cards today? I doubt that I will, but am keeping my fingers crossed just the same! ETA of postman – half an hour from now.

Part 3

Awakening

Spring 1984

Carrick

4 March 1984

Hi Cathy,

Guess you must be having kittens by now, huh? I'm really, <u>really</u> sorry it took so long for me to write back, but I honestly didn't get around to it. Last week every spare second had to be spent in catching up on me Law for a test. If it's any consolation to youse, I got good marks, so your sacrificing of not getting a letter contributed to it!

Any road, how are ya? Things are as usual over 'ere. Maw and Paw are as daft as ever. No, we've got no pussies jumping in the kitchen window any more but we have adopted a new black kitten. He's really adorable (but a bit skinny). Actually we haven't named him* yet. How would you like the honour of doing so?

The little fella next door (Stephen who's about 2½) is nuts about him. He calls pussy the goggy (or maybe it's doggy!). Stephen is <u>really</u> wild but is so cute; he's adorable. Maybe I'll change my mind when summer comes and he starts jumping on our prize dahlias and takes a fancy to pelting stones at the big girl next door!

How's your little charge? I'm really delighted you're getting on so well with him. Nothing like the auld maternal instinct, huh?!

By the way, guess who got married yesterday, P— T—. She married the baby's father. Her father wasn't at the wedding, I heard, 'cos himself and the missus have finally split up and he was afraid if he went that she'd create a scene and spoil the day for everyone. Talk about *Dallas*, huh? I saw S— N— up town last

---

* The cat turned out to be female so the pronoun changes further along!

Wednesday pushing a pram. She looked <u>so</u> old and so, well, MARRIED-LOOKING that I had to look twice before I recognised her. Also I saw a photo (which I've passed on to you) of Mary Hurton's wedding. Is she the same Mary Hurton that you used to talk of? The fella's not bad-looking, huh?

Nearly got a heart attack this morning. I went over town with Anne-Marie after Mass. We went into Coghlans where I weighed myself. Guess what. I've gained nearly a half stone – 8 stone 6 pounds. There's no sense to me, though; I'm gone stark raving mad about choccy, and chippies, and crispies and . . . at this rate, I'll get no summer clothes to fit moi (which incidentally are fantastic in Waterford – with fantastic prices too). I guess, though, that the shock didn't have much effect, as I've already eaten an ice cream, bar of choccy, some bonbons and Rolos since dinner and it's just three o'clock now! Actually, I think my maw's half to blame as she loads up the drawers with the aforementioned nasties and I, being the obliging, non-wasteful soul that I am must eat 'em!

I wonder did you hear anything on your news over there about Ann Lovett? No? Well, there's been this big row over here about it and everyone's been talking about it since. You see there was this girl called Ann Lovett in Granard, Co. Longford who was fifteen. There about a month ago some schoolboys found her in a grotto to Our Lady, having just given birth to a baby boy. Both mother and baby died later. Immediately, all of the holier-than-thous went preaching. Nuala Fennell* ordered a full investigation as to how such a thing could happen in 1984. All the journalists and reporters went snooping – big headlines, photos, the works. It

* Women's Affairs minister.

d her in a grou...
...ing just given birth
...boy. Beth mother and
...ster. Immediately, all
...on-thous went preaching
...ordered a Bull
...to have such a thing
in 1984. All the
...reporters went snooping
...es, photos, the works.
...r parents knew nothing
...teachers and nuns in
...nothing (though she was
...school up to the birth!!)
...ade her friends swear
...anyone. A big furore
...consolation to the 15 year
...little son, or indeed to
the next unmarried mother
...Actually, I met Sr.
...on the bus one evening
...

seemed her parents knew nothing about it. Her teachers and nuns in school knew nothing (though she was still attending school up to the birth!) and she'd made her friends swear not to tell anyone. A big furore but little consolation to the fifteen-year-old or her little son, or indeed to the next unmarried mother.

Actually, I met Sister E— on the bus one evening. She wanted to know what we (as students) thought about it all. Then she went on to say how the schools do their best to educate about sex, etc. All I could do was listen. I couldn't spoil her illusions!

Things seem to be going from bad to worse in Irish society at the moment. Just two weeks ago Maurice was telling me that there had been three suicides in Charleville alone the previous week. One fifteen-year-old boy who had been suspended from school for having a flick knife was so afraid to tell his parents that he went round asking his friends about the best way to commit suicide. Thinking it was a joke, they all contributed to the banter. But no one was laughing when they found him next day with his head blown off. Apparently, he had tied the trigger of his father's shotgun to his toe and . . .

In Cappoquin, a fifteen-year-old girl left her books in the study hall, along with a suicide note, and went and jumped off a bridge!

Anyway, on a brighter note – I finally phoned Sue. She seems to be having a whale of a time. Even had a certain young gentleman up to stay the weekend. She didn't say much else (actually the auld cow in the telephone exchange had her waxy little ear to our conversation) but promised she'd write to me. She said something about you having enough info about her goings-on to hang her. Pass it on to moi, and I'll look for a tree!

Got a lovely letter from Wendy. I was delighted. She was asking about youse and I told her all the spicy bits (what spicy bits? I dunno, you'd better get crackin' and do sommat spicy!).

Oh, surprise, surprise, Y— eventually had her bambino, her petit chou, a little girl who's supposed to be absolutely adorable with tufts of black hair. Guess she was worth waiting for after all!

Nanny is bent with bad arthritis at the moment and to crown it all the doctors have discovered she has a prolapsed womb (wouldn't wonder after nearly twenty kids and no medical care of any description).

Now about college. Guess who went on strike on 13 Feb? You see there was this huge student protest over the refusal of Barry Desmond* to allow students be assessed for medical cards independently of their parents. Some students neither live at home nor have seen their parents for years. So, that Monday morning we were down in the Barracks† as usual when at around 12.05 the student union pres. John Doyle, came in and said that a strike had been called at a meeting in the college, that 1,500 students had marched to the Barracks to bring us out too, and that they were now locked out ('cos the college had phoned the Barracks, who closed the gates). We marched outside, climbed through the door and a big cheer went up from the crowd outside. We all marched to the Mall (receiving odd stares from passers-by) amid chants of 'What do we want? Medical cards. When do we want 'em? Now!' And 'Barry – Out, Barry – Out, Barry, Barry, Barry, Out, Out, Out!' I've never enjoyed myself so much. It was great. There was a sit-in on the Mall outside the Health Board offices, blocking traffic, etc. We

* Health minister.
† Home of the accountancy class, a former army barracks over a mile from the main campus.

thought it might get hot (as the guards began to be drafted in) so we slinked off – shame! During the strike I overheard one guy calling another 'comrade'! Anyway, victory is ours – as the slogan in the canteen says. The whole question has been resolved and the students in Mountjoy (who were jailed for sit-ins) have been released.

To let you in on a secret, I've a giant-sized crush on a guy in the class. I don't know why – he's not over-dishy, can be very rude, sometimes uses atrocious language, etc., but somehow I can't stop thinking about him. In some ways, he'd remind you of Catherine – a dark stranger, very profound – but he's even wittier than Tricia Colleton. He's an answer for everything and everyone. The same guy hardly knows I exist, I'd say, and at the end of the year he'll be returning home and I'll never see him again – boo-hoo ... Ah, well, c'est la vie.

You wanted to know a bit about my course. Well, I'll be two years in Waterford, during which I'll sit my Prof. 1 and Prof. 2 exams. Then I'll go into the office for four years and sit Prof. 3 and Final Admitting. Then I'll be qualified (some hope! The failure rate is 53 per cent of all final students) and I'll have the letters ACA after my name. (Taking into account that, by the time I'll have done all that study, I'll have been driven to the bottle, the ACA could well stand for A CHRONIC ALCOHOLIC!)

The big news in Carrick at the moment is the opening of Liam Bennett's new shopping centre (on the site of the old Ormond Hall). I've sent you a piccy. It's a strange monstrosity! Brendan Grace (Bottler) opened it officially last Thursday. It has a coffee shop so that's another place to add to your list of places we'll have to visit when you come home again. (You are coming home again?!) Actually, Paddy Farrell is having a double dose of kittens and canaries 'cos he's afraid he'll lose his customers to Bennett or to Tesco (who've just opened in Clonmel).

Listen, I'd better shurrup as I've got the most excruciating pain in my hand (no doubt you've one in your head!). Also I want to watch *MT USA* on TV which is three hours of non-stop music videos and pop music (actually quite good, too!). Maw sends you her love; the coffee-table is polished every day. (I actually do me homework on it and we play the odd game of cards!) Hope this letter makes up for the delay.

Write again soon. Slán.

Lots of love,
Mary

PS Like me paper? Bought it just for ya and it's nearly all gone. You'll have me broke!

Trégunc

Saturday, 10 March 1984

Dear Mary,

You'd be surprised (or maybe you wouldn't!) at the number of names you've been called this past week, as the postman passed day after day, without leaving your customary parcel behind. I was beginning to think you'd never again write, when hope was finally restored today and I was able to pass my lunch eating and reading at the same time!

The combination of these two resulted in everybody having a good giggle as I tried to wipe magret de canard au poivre vert from one of the pages! By the way how did you get away with paying 30p when I generally pay 40p for a package of half that weight?!

Interruption No. 1 already! Bye!

I'm now continuing this letter three and a half hours later. Y'see, I'd a few little things to do. First of all, this morning Viv asked me if I'd mind nicking a few flowers from the local vacant houses, as they're having a social in the restaurant tonight and she wants to do it up a bit. Then François wanted me to collect some seaweed for the decoration of the dishes.

Do you know what 'fruits de mer' is? No? Well, it's a big plate and you put piles of crabs, mussels, lobster kinda things, and piles of other varied shellfish on it. But before you do all that you've to cover the plate with fucus vesiculosus, etc. It's then garnished with very thin slices of lemon. The whole thing looks really gorgeous when it's done, I must admit that, even though I don't like shellfish.

(There was this Irish guy who came to eat here during the summer and he chose 'fruits de mer'. Afterwards he complained to François that the SALAD had not been seasoned enough. The bloody idiot went and ate the seaweed.)

As well as all that, Thomas wanted to go for a walk. Hence, I combined the three chores. By the way, I didn't spend 3½ hours at the beach. When I came home, I had a coffee, as is customary at four thirty, and then I finished my book (reading one, that is, not writing it!).

And guess what, I actually got to talk to somebody! Yippee! It was a woman (forty-ish) who was collecting sea shells with two of her kids. The little fella knew Thomas, consequently we got talking. She was a real chatterbox, for which I was very grateful. Have you any idea how absolutely BORING, NERVE-RACKING and INTOLERABLE it is to see the same people day after day after day? Any little 'bonjour' out of the ordinary is really marvellous.

And while speaking of out of the ordinary, I made my debut in French society at the Grand Bal Masqué à Trégunc about a fortnight ago. I went with Alain's parents, Marcel and Marie-Thérèse, both of whom are forty-ish, as was nearly everyone else there, except for those who were eleven or twelve years old. There were a number of my contemporaries there, none of whom approached me, not surprisingly as human nature is the same everywhere and those in groups tend to stay in their respective groups. The fancy dress was fairly good and prizes were given at the end of the evening, by which stage I was three-quarters dead from the coldness, the cig. smoke, not to mention the boredom. There was one guy in a purple sheet who headed our way more than once but by 10 p.m. I was in such a bad humour I said, 'No'! Perhaps if he hadn't been wearing so much make-up (merely for disguise, I assure you!) and if I'd seen what I somehow guessed to be a good-looking face, I might have felt different. Anyway, even if none of us enjoyed ourselves, I'm still glad that I'd the experience of going.

The French version of *Non-stop Pop* was devoted to women and female groups last night. But I think somebody somewhere slipped up, because a video clip of Culture Club was included!

The subject of Sue . . . well, some of her activities would shock you to death! It's a different fella every day of the week. Lucky there's so many of them in college. Her cohabitants sound just as bad, and what's more, there's five male nuts living almost beside them. I think they'll be hanging red lights up in that estate one of these days. I quite envy her really. She seems to be the typical college student and living life to its full. And you don't seem to be doing too badly in that field yourself!

Is your mother reading this? Can I continue? Well, I'm going to leave that subject for a while as I've to go searching thru my archives as you neglected to give the name of your crush!

I expect that by the time you get this letter, Cath C will have given you the photos taken at Christmas. Can you be an angel and send them back the next time you write as they belong to Celia? I've two photos to take on a reel of twenty-four. I should get them developed in the next fortnight, and if they turn out well, I'll send them on to you. I think the majority are of Thomas. Unfortunately, I didn't get to take any of Yvan or Bruno (Chantal either!). But then I couldn't very well say, 'Excuse me, but can I take your photo? I want to send to my friends in Ireland and make them jealous when they see what kinda company I keep every day.' For one thing, I'd have an awful problem trying to translate all of that!

I may have been a little bowled over by Yvan's good looks when I first arrived here, but after six months, I know him a bit better. Okay, he's got fantastic dark brown eyes, great sense of humour and charm but, my God, is he a bore! He seems to think that the world turns on his bloody culinary skill! Talk about vanity and big-headedness. He even takes photos of his creations! And he never shuts up about his mother, brothers, sisters, son, wife, divorce, car, mouldy apartment (shared with Chantal) and father (RIP since Christmas).

Bruno is much nicer. He's not as good-looking (or at least I think not) but he's ten times funnier, a terrific actor, the kinda person you can feel at ease with. You know you can be yourself, and not ashamed or shy of what you are. He makes me laugh. He was on two weeks' holidays and, boy, was the place <u>dull</u>! Please don't read anything that isn't there into this. I've met his girlfriend two or three times. She's just terrific. <u>Very</u> chic. Kinda smallish and plumpish and blondish. Totally uninhibited, not a bit shy, a perfect partner of Bruno. In a word, she's FRENCH. She works (most surprisingly) in a paper and paint shop.

It's around 6.30 p.m. now. Viv is doing herself up for the meal this evening. It's a crowd of politicians coming for an annual meal, I believe. Viv never wears the waitress traditional apron. Just as I finished the last paragraph, she called me. She's just put on her wedding dress. It still looks great after twelve years. It's not a lacy thing. I can't really describe the material, sorta linen, I suppose, with embroidery. It's really beautiful and has class. But it doesn't really fit any more. She was five months pregnant when she got married, y'see. She'd only put on the dress to please the kids. She went down to show it to François in the restaurant. I'm going to wait until she comes back up to finish this paragraph . . . Ah, there she is. Being his usual unromantic self – a typical hubby, in fact – he said nothing, just made a face. Must go now for supper.

11 p.m. same day

As you can see there is no rhyme or reason to this letter. At the moment, I'm sorta watching a Johnny Hallyday concert made in Nashville. François and Vivianne are still working downstairs. Delphine and Thomas are in bed. Chrystelle, as usual, fell asleep on the couch. I don't really like Johnny, but now he's singing a soft romantic song and I feel very lonely. Songs like that shouldn't be listened to when you're alone. There should be a fire roaring, wine glasses sparkling, a fluffy sheepskin rug with piles of cushions and a gorgeous hunk . . . Viv says I'm too romantic and she's right, I suppose! But what other way can one be at almost nineteen years of age?

Your newly acquired cat – well, how about a really original name like 'Blackie'? The cat here is fantastic. A huge big grey called Mimique (another suggested name), who got into a fight a while ago and tore a hole in his leg. I almost cried when I saw it. They all tease me here because I'm crazy about the cat, but can't stand the dog. Dadouche is a fat, lazy, smelly, greedy,

dirty spaniel sorta thing. She eats anything that waits for her –
except cabbage. François says it's because whenever she comes
near me I always say, 'Shoo, Dadouche!' Get it?! Seriously, I
think 'Miou-miou' is a lovely name (you say 'Mew-Mew').
She's a French actress that I can't stand. She's the type who
doesn't give the wardrobe department many problems, if you
know what I mean! But I still like the name!

I know what you mean about the fantastic clothes for the
summer. I haven't actually seen them in the shops yet, but a
few catalogues arrived here and the stuff is out of this world.
Prices aren't too bad either. But I've got the old problem, i.e.
I find size twelve much better than size sixteen! But this year,
I've got something to work towards. It'll be worthwhile the
starvation. I am absolutely determined to look presentable
on the beach!

Speaking of which, what've you given up for Lent? I'm
going to be really tough on myself this year – jam, cake, etc.,
and hardest of all, cheese, which is gorgeous here! Mind you,
I was at Marie-Thérèse's on Thursday, and had both jam and
cake. Y'see, she'd made it herself and if I hadn't eaten 'em
she'd have been very hurt . . .

Incidentally, I felt very homesick looking at the catalogues.
They brought back memories of when I used to plague your
house on Saturdays, and after dinner we'd have coffee and
biscuits and piles of more calories and look at all the fantastic
clothes and wish we were rich (sometimes I feel like a really
old little lady – with a yellow canary – writing my memoirs. I
can't help being soppy – excuse me).

At 00.06 hrs telly is finished so I've put on my tapes – Julio
Iglesias – which reminds me of my next topic. He says he

loves Paris every moment of the year – because his MOTHER lives there! (Ah, now he's singing 'Feelings' and I'm really going to cry. I taped the record I bought Celia for Christmas.)

Well, where was I? Oh, yes, not in Paris. I think Viv's sister's plans have changed and so no Paris for me. As a matter of fact, she never even phoned to tell us I couldn't go. Next time I see 'er I'll give 'er a black eye! So, I think the only way I'll get there is under my own steam (and no smart cracks about me looking like a steam engine, okay?). Maybe the two of us will make it there together!

I wrote to Catherine last week and as far as I remember I was in a very peculiar mood. Can you apologise to her for me for all the peculiarities in my letter? (I suppose when I write to Sue next week I'll ask her to apologise to you for the same reason. Talk about a vicious circle!)

Sue twisted a few arms, and as a result a few of her NIHE friends wrote a few notes at the end of her last letter. As previously mentioned, they sound rather peculiar. But one of the guys, I think it's a John, I'm too lazy to go looking up her letter now, appears very nice – you know the way you try to guess by the writing. Mind you, I hope they don't try to divine my character from my writing. If they do, they'll run like the hounds of hell (one of Nanny's inexplicable sayings!) every time they see me approaching!

I must say, old chap (bowler hat, briefcase, brolly under one arm and *The Times* under the other!), your granny really seems to have hit a tough spot at the moment. What between arthritis and God only knows what else. Talk about being unlucky. Granny Gough didn't build her house on a fairy fort or anything, did she?

Well, to date, I've apologised for content, atrociousness of writing and my letter to Catherine. So now I'm going to apologise for my paper. I feel all the more ashamed of it as I glance back at your lovely stuff. Fact of the matter is I write to so many people at regular (you, Sue, Eleanor, Catherine and Glen) and irregular (Daddy, Celia, Anne M, aunts in England, Mag, Joan and so on) intervals that if I were to buy decent writing paper, well, I'd have to take out a mortgage on me jewellery! As it is, I'm stone broke buying stamps. And I've almost run out of typing paper – courtesy of Celia at Christmas.

Ah! Meanie, you did the crossword in the *Messenger*!

Wednesday, 14 March

Hi again, I'm determined to get this letter finished today and hopefully, if someone goes to Trégunc, posted tomorrow. Anyway, at last something has happened, i.e. got a phone call in the middle of the day Monday. First thought was 'My God, the IRA has blown up the house in Glen', or some similar catastrophe! Anyway, it turned out that it was just somebody who wanted me to give English lessons to her daughter. Yippee! At last!

So anyway, I went today between eleven and twelve. They live about two miles up the road and Marie-Claude, the oldest daughter (twenty), came to pick me up in the car. Anne is about eleven, and seems bright enough. But in the schools over here, there's a little exam in every subject once a fortnight. Strict control is kept of all such notes, and at the end of the year, to pass into the next higher class, an overall average of

12/20 is required. Quite a good idea, I think. Anyway, Anne has something like 11.3. So she wants to push it up a bit.

Afterwards, I was talking to their mother, who appears really nice, and she suggested that myself and Marie-Claude (I think that's her name) get together and go out a few times. Naturally, I was thrilled. Somebody my own age at last. And so now, even though there's nothing definite planned, well, there's something to look forward to.

But to be perfectly honest, I'm scared stiff. You see, she's really glamorous, and young, and typically French. Beside her, I feel about ninety, and very old-fashioned and dumpy and all those other horrible adjectives. So I suppose I'll have to dye my hair carrot red and eat nothing but the latter for a month before I feel comfortable beside her. Anyway, I'm going back there again next Wednesday for Anne's lesson. Their house – FANTASTIC in a word!

D'you know the song 'Mrs Robinson'? Can you explain it to me? I get the impression that it's an alcoholic mother, but I'm not sure.

At the moment, we're waiting for the doctor to see Thomas, who's got a high temperature again. I'm not surprised, really. Vivianne dressed him in shorts last week. Okay, the sun was shining, but at the same time it was very cold. But every time the kids take a temp of 1° more than it should be, she immediately phones for the doctor. I suppose better safe than sorry, but at the same time, she'll soon be able to open up a drug counter in the restaurant! Luckily enough, their insurance reimburses every penny.

I'm going to go and look at your old letters now in an attempt to discover this Romeo. Back in a sec . . .

Aha! Found him! I can imagine somebody very tall, well-built, NOT Mr Muscle. With dark hair that always flops into his very brown humorous eyes. And a generous mouth that reveals perfect white teeth when he smiles. No, that is not copied word for word from a Mills & Boon. I made it all up my little self!

But rereading your letter, I see that he's really not all that marvellous in the appearance category, and is not an angel either. Why are we attracted to other people? I cannot understand it myself. Okay, if he's a Robert Redford type, okay, that's comprehensible, but why do we get crushes on guys that are just plain and ordinary? But, then, I never was great at chemistry!

Personally, I think life'd be as miserable as hell if we didn't have crushes on boys. What utter monotony and misery that would be. You know when I do the ironing now, I compose letters home to you to be posted in the summer which are as follows:

Dear Mary/Sue/Eleanor/Catherine, Please excuse me for not writing for the past two months, but between Jean-Paul, Marc, Yann, X, Y and Z, I've been terribly busy. And when I had a minute to myself, well, I was too tired to write. You know how fatiguing it can be, dancing 'til four in the morning, and then, well, the return trips in the red sports cars can be SO exhausting . . .

Well, maybe you know yourself what a horrible bore ironing is, especially a minimum of two hours a day. I mean you have to do some kind of mind travelling if you want to stay sane! And, you never know, perhaps my dream will come true someday (and no smart comments about cows sprouting wings and flying!).

I've just written, with a lot of help from Viv, a rather nasty letter to the teachers of my correspondence course. In the books, they tell you 'Do this, like this.' You spend three hours a day typing arthritis into your fingers, only to get an exercise back, with red biro all over it saying, 'Why did you do this like this? You're supposed to do it like that!' So now I'm thoroughly browned off it. The whole thing is very discouraging.

How did it feel to be on strike? I bet you were disappointed they didn't call in the riot squad with nerve gas and batons and all that! Speaking of strikes – the whole of France is in an uproar because of them. They're everywhere (sounds rather frightening and sinister, doesn't it?). Even the Paris–Nice bike race ran into some trouble. I believe a few of the cyclists got and gave a few wallops. Let me ask you a serious question – do you think Sean Kelly knows how to smile?

Anyway, hoping to hear from you soon, love to all, write <u>very</u> soon.

Tons of love,
Catherine

PS Have an appointment to get me goggles changed. But it's ages away – 11 April. Had to wait for about six weeks.

PPS What's happening in *Dynasty*?

Carrick

Monday, 26 March 1984

Dear Cathy,

I'm writing this here letter on a Monday morning. Now, I hear you ask yourself, wot's yer wan doing home on a Monday morning? Has she been thrown out, expelled, even? Well, 'pour tranquilliser' your beating 'coeur', we're on holidays, actually, for two weeks. Not much of a holiday really, 'cos I've got <u>tons</u> of study to do (and that's just the weight of the books!). Our accounts lecturer wanted us to get up at <u>6.30 a.m.</u> to study, just like she did when she was going. Might explain the cut of her – she missed out on her beauty sleep!

Now for a bit of news . . . I guess you're gonna be quite disappointed really 'cos nothin' scandalous happened since my last letter. No really juicy bits of gossip.

Oh, hang on, I just thought of something. Remember the pub at the end of the Parish Height going up towards the Friary? Well, this guy went in there last week with a knife and threatened the woman there. Luckily some knight in shining armour came to the rescue but not before she had suffered a nasty shock. Honestly, Kitty dear, what is the world coming to! That didn't happen in our day! And as for the youth of today . . .

By the way we christened the pussy Mimi. Maw found Mew-Mew too hard to say, what with the false teeth and all! So Mimi it is to be.

Cheryl was in to see me on Sunday (with her little sister Kate). Her chances of going to Canada are becoming slimmer and slimmer 'cos they can't get a visa for her. Therefore, she's thinking of doing an AnCO course instead. Actually, I was asking her about Dominic ('cos I haven't seen him yet) and she was telling me about his lovely Roman nose (yes – nose!), which she adores! I'm sure if he had heard her describing his NOSE (shape, structure, colour!) he'd have shrivelled up and died. Anyway, the next day I couldn't prevent myself from staring at his baby brother who's on the same bus as me to see if he had one. Honest, he must think I'm loony.

So do you by this stage, I guess.

To get back to the people next door. Yes, Stephen is Anthony D's nephew. Actually he's really cute – Stephen, that is! You see, usually he plays ball in the back garden and it sometimes comes over into our place. Every time Maw hands it back to him she says, 'You're a good boy, aren't you, Stephen?' To which he modestly replies, 'Yes, I am'! Anyway this morning, Maw was hanging out the clothes when in came the ball. She threw it back to Stephen. He stood there eyeing her solemnly for a few seconds 'cos she hadn't said anything, and then he announced, 'I'm a good boy!' and galloped off, leaving Maw in the stitches.

There go the county council men in their noisy digger again. (Maw calls it a gusher or a guzzar!) Anyway, at the moment, they're outside doing the road, cleaning shores etc. ('cos yesterday we had torrential rain and everywhere got soaked and flooded). I looked out the window this morning to see one of them holding a shovel (breast-feeding it!) while two more stood beside him looking into a hole. Some things never change, huh?

My da has been in bed all last week 'cos of the terrible flu going around. Niamh had it for four days and so did half of my class.

Do you remember Helen who was in our class for French? Well, her mother died yesterday of cancer. I meant to tell you about her before. Last summer she went for an operation for gall stones and when they operated they found she had cancer of the liver. They couldn't do much for her. She was getting progressively worse. At Christmas Niamh met Helen with the two younger kids. All they were worried about was seeing the crib. Helen started crying. After Christmas her mother got worse. She was in a lot of pain as the drugs were wearing off. She couldn't take any food 'cos the cancer had spread to her stomach. Since they couldn't do any more for her they left her home. Helen (who was in Mater Dei) came home to nurse her. She died yesterday . . . at forty years of age. Strange world, isn't it?

To change from this depressing subject, I've given up sweets for Lent and I'm going <u>mad</u>. Guess what else I'm doing. I've made a promise to make the sign of the cross every time I pass Piltown church, regardless of what anyone says. I know I'm nuts, ya needn't tell me. I went to Mass a few mornings in the lecture theatre. The priest is really nice. Father Pat he's called and is really funny. He ran out of communion one day and said, 'Sorry about that. Just shows ya I'm not as good as my master at making the food go further but I'm working on it!'

What sort of catalogues have you got? Any chance of sending to moi? I'd love to see one if it wouldn't cost you a bomb in postage. Talking about postage, do you have to pay extra postage on my letters? If you do I'll go down and punch Michael O'Donnell on the nose, 'cos he puts on the stamps for Maw, whose job it is to post these masterpieces.

I was delighted your last letter was handwritten (though if my poor eyes could talk . . .): it adds a piece of 'je ne sais quoi'. Also, don't worry about the paper. As I said before I'd read it if it were on loo paper. Actually, I heard about this from a priest: he buys a newspaper and writes his letter in the margins and between the lines so as to save postage as it costs less to post newspapers! You should do the same!

What were you saying about our National Hero, Sean Kelly? How dare ya, ya hussy? Where's your sense of patriotism? Your civic spirit?

Actually I agree with youse but I think he's getting better. They interviewed him here on the telly recently and I was more than surprised that he was as good as he was. He was actually well able to explain himself.

I saw Tina on the bus one evening. We had an open week in the WRTC so Greenhill had a day off (though Tina went shopping in Waterford instead and bought nothing). She's still the same Tina. She looked fantastic. I think, though, she may be sorry she went back as now she's not even sure if she wants to teach. As well as that, she was saying the competition will be just as stiff this time round.

Talking about competition: Bank of Ireland has opened its ranks again. They have thirty full-time posts and a good few part-time posts. A lot of the lads below* applied, so did Tina and Margaret Bartley. They were all called to Dublin at different dates to do an aptitude test. Guess how many applied – SIX THOUSAND (yep, 6,000). Imagine you have one chance in 200 of getting a full-time job!

H— has finished up and has left WRTC. She's starting nursing

---

* Students from Greenhill.

next week. Let's hope she gets on well. Listen, hang on a minute. I'm gonna shift myself upstairs 'cos the radio has just been turned on and I can't concentrate!

Hello again. Now to the real purpose of this letter, old chappie. I read with <u>amazement</u> the part of your letter which said you're scared stiff of going out with Marie-Claude 'cos (gulp for breath) you feel about ninety. And old-fashioned? And dumpy? Nuts and fiddlesticks, I say, old chappie! Have you honestly looked at those photos I'm sending back to you? All I can say is that if you only looked half as good, Marie-Claude would have to beware. I'm not joking. I got the photos from Catherine in college so Niamh got to see 'em. She was stunned and staggered by, as she said, the 'definite improvement'! She said you exuded such poise, grace, dignity and radiance that she couldn't believe it was you. Now I tell you, if you can get such rave comments from Niamh you've crowned it ('cos she's really critical). I myself never saw you looking so dashing and debonair. All I can say is that if France does that to a person, then I'm coming out when my next grant instalment comes through. (How does Paris in the spring strike you?)

There was I in the depths of despair having seen those wonderful photos of you, while I eyed me mutt in the mirror – the chin like drumlin country, the shapeless mop, the dry, down-turning mouth – with mounting distaste, and along comes your letter, which says you think <u>you</u> were ninety. Imagine how <u>I</u> felt! So now, old chappie, enuf of this poppycock, I say. You're looking fab (and the blouse is gorgeous – any chance of it?) and you're <u>the</u> most interesting person I know. Why else d'ya think I'd be giving myself writer's cramp with these letters? No joking, when Paw saw the photos he said you looked like a film star (and he didn't mean

Fozzie Bear either!). By the way, the fellas saw it too and thought you were gorgeous.

Now to my crush. SHANE, you think it is. Ya nitwit, it isn't Shane. I nearly died while I read it and then I nearly had convulsions when I read your describing how ya thought he'd look – tall (ha!), dark hair (ha-ha), brown humorous eyes (haw-haw, hee-hee). He is none of the above.

The heartthrob in my life has a very ordinary-sounding name for a most extraordinary fella! I guess he really isn't all that bad-looking. But you can understand I can't judge that objectively. My crush is becoming a bit squashed 'cos really he keeps rejecting me. Sob! Sob! I mean, there I go falling at his feet – and he just steps over me! I offer him a bit of me apple and he says no. I offer to lend him some paper and he says he's already got some! Seriously, though, he must think I'm the dullest, the thickest and the most boring person around 'cos I never know what to say to him and end up looking a full fool. Ya know how terrifying witty people can be!

He is really something but a relationship with him would be out of the question as he'd walk all over me, have me for breakfast and regurgitate me for dinner (how's that for symbolism?). Another guy is really nice, though, and I like him a lot but I haven't got a crush on him. He's really witty too but knows where to draw the line. He is a gentleman in every sense of the word and he'll make someone very happy someday 'cos he makes you feel like a princess instead of dumpy Mary, Joan or Biddy.

Now to my problem. Honestly, Cathy, I'm seriously getting worried. I may be flattering myself but I think one of the guys fancies me. It's really quite embarrassing. He persists in sitting beside me (thus depriving everyone else of the chance!). Okay, it was funny at the beginning but now . . . Take last week: myself and Nuala decided we'd go to Paddy Browne's for lunch. We were on our own, when suddenly in he walked having followed us all the way. Then he wouldn't leave until I left too! A few days later, all the fellas were going down to play snooker. He came over and asked me would I come with them while all the other fellas stood looking in amazement. I was the only girl in the group, which was pretty embarrassing. Needless to say, I didn't go.

Then last week I moved desk and the fellas got on to me so much about rejecting him and <u>he</u> looked so desolate that I had to move back. Last Thursday night he took this girl to the disco and Niamh maintains he did it to make me jealous. Dear Aunty Katie, HELP. I mean, I don't want to hurt his feelings or anything but he's too much of a boy. He's only seventeen (listen to Methuselah speaking!) and he seems a little sheltered by his mammy (incidentally he brought in photos of his mammy to show <u>to me</u>, so that looks serious, huh?!). He tries to tell jokes (which I don't find funny!). I'm going spare!

We voted for a new union last Thursday. I felt all 'growed up' as I cast my vote. You see they (Liam and Shane) were only going for a laugh, just to put up funny posters.

My favourite song at the moment is 'Hello' by Lionel Richie. I understand fully about the fireside, sparkling wine, sheepskin rugs and – nearly forgot – the hunk. I think both of us are incurable romantics and I hope we never change.

How did Paddy's Day go? I can just imagine you going around

singing 'Hail Glorious (hiccup) St Patrick (hiccup), Dear
Saint (hiccup) of our (hiccup) Isle'. I was going to send you a
sprig of shamrock but I guess your grandmaw did that. I don't
know wot it is about Paddy's Day but it always gives me a lump
in my throat! The Mass I went to was all in Irish. Children with
badges and green ribbons; parents with clumps of shamrock,
to which half of the field was still attached. Had a fab dinner
of yummy roast beef (the blessings of God on St Patrick
anyway).

Dominic McGlinchey, the most wanted man in Ireland,
was caught that day too. Now the guards can be sure that they
won't be robbed of their uniforms again (as he did three times,
leaving them standing in their undies by the roadside!). He was
caught in Co. Clare and Killian said there was no truth in the
rumour that he was to be the Grand Marshal in the Ennis
parade!

After dins me maw and I went to the Carrick parade. Met Mary
Meagher (an old neighbour from Mass Road). There were tears in
me eyes as we swapped stories of Mass Road – hens with 'gammy'
legs, cabby houses, plates of bacon and cabbage – oh, for the days
of yore. The parade was useless except for the Macra cow (see
Carrick Opinion for picture). Guess who was pulling its tail. Only
Monie May. Poor bruvver was the only fella in the Civil Defence
contingent. We went to the park then to see the Irish dancing but
it was so cold we came home via the Clinic (I only had Cidona!).
By the way, the new chipper-cum-restaurant is open. The smell
coming from the place was DIABOLICAL but the food is supposed
to be OKAY. Also, rumour has it that there's an absolute dream of
a hunk behind the counter who's guaranteed to turn your knees
to jelly.

Listen, I'd better shurrup if I want to get this letter in the post today. Hope you're keeping well and all that jazz.

Best wishes and lots of love,
Mary

PS I've just read about Annette and Nicola Cleary doing so well with their classical music. I've sent it on to you.

The usual dull boring dump
in the middle of nowhere

A Saturday night in April

Dear Mary,

Someday I'm going to make a resolution to write letters
which do not contain an apology. All of that, however, is in
the unseeable future, and for the moment I hope you accept
my apologies for not writing to you sooner. But over the past
week, I've been too busy, not to mention not being in the
humour of uniting ink and paper.

And while accepting my apologies, please accept all my
'thank yous' as well for your pressie, which arrived today. As
it's almost 11 p.m. my normally drowsy brain has more or less
completely dozed off and so the only appropriate phrase –
'It's what I always wanted!' – while being VERY TRUE is
somewhat unoriginal. But, honestly, I'm not just saying that
to please you. I really did need a gold chain, and the thing
(haven't a clue what it's called!) hanging on it is very unusual
and eye-catching in this neck of the woods. And the proof of
that is that it sparked off a conversation with Yvan, who
happened to be sitting beside me when the postman came at
dinner time. I sorta hung around the kitchen this evening
(have you any idea how bloody messy it is hanging around a
kitchen?) and sponged a cookery lesson out of him, and
learnt the French version of making a madeira cake (which
somewhat disappointingly resembles the Irish method – only
there's no comparison between Sister Thérèse and Yvan!).

But anyway the message of all the above pointless

rambling is just to say thanks for thinking of me, and I wish I could be with you on the 11th.

Let's see, what have I in the way of news? Oh, yes, got me peepers tested last night. Went to the eye specialist yesterday evening in Concarneau. Secretary was a right sour ole bitch. So, I was expecting this grumpy ancient grandpa to appear out of the office. Instead this young (late twenties), handsome guy materialises. Boy, was I stunned. And the surprise of seeing him combined with his space-age equipment left me speechless for all of five minutes.

God, when I think of the optician at home and the dartboard-like chart pinned to the back of a door of a little kitchen of a room! Anyway, I won't go into all the complicated details of the examination. To tell the truth I was so mesmerised by his gorgeous big brown eyes, which were only centimetres from my own, that I hardly noticed anything else. (Viv came with me in case I'd have language problems. And later she embarrassed the life out of me as we were eating back in the restaurant and she started blabbing on about 'bouche à bouche'. I sorta turned the colour of Heinz's tomato sauce, dug a hole in the floor and slid into it!)

But they've a bizarre system here. The guy who tests your eyes doesn't actually sell the frames or arrange for the mounting of the glass. He just writes the lenses required on a piece of paper and then you go to an optician who sells you the frames and arranges to have them fitted. So, the test itself cost me £10. Then today I went and after much headshaking finally chose my future goggles. The frames cost me £45! And the glass for each lens £23. Grand total over £100 – a month's wages. Admittedly, I'm having the lenses tinted, but that only costs £10 more than buying the little sunglasses things you can buy separately, which are very ugly, badly fitting and are generally in your bedroom while you're squinting on the beach!

But I think if I didn't get new glasses, and soon at that, I'd have ended up walking under a car. I'm almost as blind as a bat, and lately I've been getting terrible headaches. So even though I've already cried an ocean over my month's work, well, I suppose it's money well spent!

As they had two weeks' holidays (again!) from school, François brought the two girls to see his parents in Paris. Initially, I was supposed to go with them, staying at Viv's sister's place. But she couldn't provide accommodation at the time, so I'm supposed to go sometime in the next fortnight (but I doubt that I'll ever get there, except under my own steam!). The train journey'll cost me £35. So naturally I'm really annoyed I couldn't have gone with François. That'd have cost me nothing at all.

That self-same guy who was supposed to show me around in February is now supposed to take his holidays at the same time as me, and once again outline a tour of the city. But any notions I may (?) have had of a Frenchified Romeo have been quenched by a remark of Vivianne's – 'Assez moche et pas riche' (pretty ugly and not rich!). Shucks! Knowing my luck he'd end up being the reincarnation of Quasimodo. Okay, I know he was a nice 'gentil' type but, heck, what do I care about that? As I'm only going to be in his company for a week, I want somebody gorgeous-looking, debonair, rich, charming, romantic, with a small red two-seater (i.e. sports car!). Yes, you've guessed, a guy straight from M & B!

And I can't ask Vivianne what he's like, as she'll only tease me, and I did enough blushing last night to last me a lifetime! So I guess I'll have to suffer in silence.

Anyway, by this stage, I'm really too tired to do any more scribbling and my never-very-active brain is now carrying a sign, which says, 'Strike on here!' So, I'll stick my pen back in my pencil (yawn!) case, my finger on the light and telly switch and myself in my (yawn, yawn!) bed, without even bothering to stick my teeth in Steradent! Bonne nuit et à demain, ou le jour après, ou peut-être le jour après ça, si j'ai enfin un peu de chance dans ma malheureuse vie, jusqu'au jour quand tout le monde quitte Paris parce que j'y arrive.

Tuesday, 10 April

If I tell you that I'm currently on the beach sun-bathing, while over my head the sun is a round blazing ball and the 'alouettes' are singing and the sea is so bright and blue, except for the odd patches which are multi-coloured due to the surfboards with sails, will you turn bright green with envy? If I were you, I would! I just hope this fabulous weather is going to last until September!

The last time I wrote, I forgot to mention Vivianne's birthday party. She was thirty-three on 29 March. We had a fondue. 'We' were Yvan and Chantal, Bruno and Françoise, me, François and naturally enough Vivianne.

Have you ever tasted fondue? It's fabulous but it may not be your cup of tea. What you do is mix a couple of kilos of various cheeses with a litre of white wine, some garlic and a few drops of kirsch. Then you gently cook the whole thing until it's thoroughly mixed and gooey and gluey and yummy. Then you transfer your saucepan onto a small spirit fire on the table, which serves to keep the cheese melted. Everybody has special long forks, onto which you stick a piece of hard bread. You then dip that into the fondue, hoping you don't lose the bread! It's really great fun and I don't know when I laughed so much. It really was a great night. For the first time since I arrived here, I really opened up and laughed and talked and was the 'me' that you all probably know but who never left Ireland.

Maybe I was a bit tipsy, I don't know. I just know it was a great night. After dessert – a fantastic, gigantic banana split – we played a dice game. Can't remember the name now – never was much good at Chinese! But I was really delighted because I won – and by miles at that. Mind you, I'd Yvan and Chantal giving me a hand, but as I was the only novice I think that's only fair, don't you?

Monday, 16 April

I suppose by this stage, you're fit to kill me. But for probably the first time in my life, I haven't really been in the humour for writing letters. At the moment I'm once again – for a totally unknown reason – going thru that stage we all went thru this time last year and which you'll hopefully not go thru again for another few years. If you still haven't cottoned on to what I'm on about – well – I'm just simply asking myself a hundred times a day . . . 'What do you want to do with your life? Where are you going from here? Are you going to stay in France, or take the risk of giving up a "job" and try and get something else at home or in England? If you put a bomb in the washing and in the roller-iron, will Vivianne take all the decisions for you and promptly put you out of your misery? Can you stand another five months of doing nothing but ironing with a few hours of the beach in between?'

I DON'T KNOW.

As you can see, I'm in a bit (?) of a depression. I'll get all that over and done with first and then cheer you up with a bit of news. The main cause of my depression, at this very exact moment, is due to my correspondence course. I've finished the typing section, and two weeks ago started the next phase, which is totally incomprehensible. So, I'm faced with indecision at the moment and just don't know what to do. I've just written to my teacher to ask her for some advice (wish you were here!). So, I suppose I'll have to wait a couple of weeks for her reply. Anyway, enough of this unpleasant topic.

My birthday – well – the day was like any other, except brekkie started with a red package encircled by a little yellow ribbon. On tearing the paper to pieces, I found a black leather case whose insides were those very necessary items required to have wonderful nails (i.e. a manicure set, dum-dum!). So, I was delighted because yes! You've guessed! It's just what I've always wanted!

That evening, while Delphine was having her music lesson, we strolled around Concarneau and had a gawk in the shops, DIY, and an art gallery. On the way home, we stopped in at Marie-Thérèse (remember *The Good Life*? Well, MT was the model!). Anyway to celebrate she took her peach wine out of hiding. I had only a small glass of it, but even so, everything went really fuzzy and peculiar. Marcel, her husband, kept pressing me to taste his famous Norman 'Eau de Vie', and in the end, I took a teaspoon of it, and yuk! Thought the Irish version was awful, but this is worse again.

Anyway, the result of taking your advice (you told me to get sloshed!) and the mixing of my drinks seemed to act as a sleeping pill because all the next day I was as dopey as they come and, in the end, had to sleep off the effects! So, I suppose it wasn't too bad a birthday after all!

Have to go and pick the kids up from school. Will try and get back to you later!

Tuesday, 17 April

Did I already mention that I've been keeping in touch with my aunt? As you may remember, I wasn't always very popular with her before I left my native shores. I think that was because I kinda had the habit of saying what I was thinking. For some inexplicable reason this always put her back up. Anyway, in her last letter she wrote, 'At least you always said what you thought. We knew what you were thinking. I hope when you come home, you'll be able to get a job near enuf so that you can come and visit us.'

I tell ya, Molly, I was speechless. The shock of it knocked me on the flat of me back. Got a pressie off her today – shucks. In fact, it's gorgeous. A book on one of my favourite topics – cats! You should see the photos – absolutely fantastic. When I have a house/flat of my own, I might detach some of them from the book and frame them to hang 'em on the walls.

Oh, yes! You were asking about catalogues here. Well, I'd

love to send you some – but I doubt if they're much different from the ones at home.

Oh, yes, bought a pair of red trousers the other day from a guy who sells from a lorry. I think you're familiar with Sloan's? Well, same idea. The trousers cost me £20 (gasp!) but quality is terrific and, besides, I'd just received that amount from Nanny for my birthday. I bought a red and white T-shirt too. On the agenda at the moment are a pair of black or/and khaki shorts and a swimsuit.

Do you know what a 'crêperie' is? Well, if you don't, let me tell you that it's a place where they sell crêpes or pancakes. Over here they work miracles with them. They stuff 'em with eggs, tomatoes, sausages, mushrooms, bacon, bananas, apples, pineapples, whiskey, rum, etc. Well, anyway, a new crêperie was opened on Sunday night in St Phil by a friend of Viv's. So, for the first time, I got to visit one. It was certainly worth it. Started off with a cheese one, followed by a super bacon and egg, finished off with one stuffed with apples – delicious. (To heck with the calories!) And the traditional drink is cider. And as the same people happen to make their own cider, its quality equals that of the crêpes. Anyway, it was a good night – and wasn't really too dear, about £3 each.

I'm enclosing some publicity left over from last year for the restaurant. Personally, I think the standard of the paper is terrible, but I think that's due to the publishing company. The road I've added in myself in blue ink is the one that goes to the sea. Sometimes when I'm in the humour for walking, I go from here to the sea, then along the coast road to Trévignon, to the pharmacie and back to St Phil. That makes about four miles. It's a lovely walk, though. Do you think we'll ever get to do it together?

Now the subject of the comments you made in your letter about the photos. Well, the photos themselves first. I think that the camera, in an effort to apologise for all the awful uncomplimentary pictures it has taken of me over the past fifth of a century, was over-generous and too kind when it carried out its purpose at Christmas. The results did not contain my three spare tyres, dull lanky hair, double chin, etc. Therefore the pictures seen didn't represent what I actually looked like. I was really surprised and may I say pleased when I saw how well they turned out.

All of that leaves me feeling like somebody's grand-aunt beside Marie-Claude. Just the same, I've gotten to know her a little bit better now (did I mention that she gives Chrystelle maths grinds while I give Anne English ones every Wednesday morning?), and I can see that even though she puts forward a calm, sophisticated appearance, underneath it all, she's just as timid and awkward as I am. I met her on the beach one day, and we were talking for twenty minutes or so. She said she'd love to be able to work in South Africa, but to do so, perfect English is required. Personally, I think she's crazy to want to work in a country on the verge of civil war. She drowned a lot of my worries when she said my accent was nice.

(Had I mentioned I'd joined the library in Concarneau? Well, the last time I left my books on the counter, as we were in a hurry, and went looking for some to take out. One of the women working there asked the other who the books belonged to, and she replied, 'Y'know, to the girl you can never understand.' So, where does that leave my accent?)

She still hasn't invited me to go to the cinema or anything with her, and I don't expect that she will do so. Just the same, I imagine, given time, we'll become quite friendly.

By the way, I've already got a tan – in the month of April too! Bought a black low-cut swimsuit in Concarneau last night. Hope I'll soon be able to use it!

Anyway, I think this letter has dragged on enuf. It's beginning to bore you, I fear. Again, I'm sorry it took so long to put together and that it's so badly phrased, disjointed, etc., etc. I think the sun is frying my brain!

I really wish you could be here with me. It'll be great when I get home in September. We'll have to rent out the Central Grill and/or the ice-cream parlour for a week, so that we'll be able to communicate verbally.

Hoping to hear from you sooner than you heard from me. Say hello to all the gang in 63, won't you, and tell 'em 'Happy Easter' (I think Celia's going home at Easter).

Tons and tons of love,
miss you all,
Catherine

PS Be sure to keep me up-to-date on your romances. Unfortunately, not being experienced in that field <u>so far,</u> I can't give you any advice.

Also, if you see Eleanor, can you tell her that I'm still waiting for a reply to my letter of two months ago?

PPS Keep me informed on the latest goings-on of *Dynasty*, won't you?!

Carrick

Sunday, 13 May 1984

Dear Cathy,

It's me again. I'm writing this on a sunny Sunday sitting on the sofa. Maw has gone off walking, Paw is reading the paper in his corner and Martin is gone off on the twenty-mile Lions Cycling Tour. Little ole me elected to stay at home and swot but I took one look at those yucky books, those double-yucky notes and those triple-yucky hand-outs, which I should have studied months ago, and I sez to myself, 'Aaargh!' So here I am writing to youse – the salve of my conscience!

Seriously, though, I was really relieved to get your last letter. You had us all in a tizzy over here, ya know. Not a trace from you for weeks. I asked around to the others to see if they had heard a thing. Negatory on all counts. I even phoned Sue. Miss Marple never did it better. I had visions of you being kidnapped by some Bedouin on a white horse, or being gobbled up on the beach by Jaws, until sanity prevailed and I had to admit that Bedouins and sharks ain't too prevalent in Trégunc. I doubt as well if you'd protest too much about the former! (Aaargh, a wasp has just flown in the door. 'Scuse me . . .)

Anyway, to get back to your letter . . . gee, you were down in the dumps, weren't you? Ironical, isn't it? I recollect you saying the same thing to me a while back. In actual fact you said, 'Pack up your troubles etc. and smile, smile, smile.' How about me saying the same to you? A taste of your own medicine, huh? Seriously, though, I hope your spirits have lifted. <u>Believe me,</u> I know what it's like. Summer is coming and I bet you'll make lots of friends to take you out of yourself. Meanwhile I'm looking forward to September as much as you. What d'ya think I sent you the calendar for?

Talking about summer, the weather has been fantastic here too. We had a great Easter. I got a sort of a tan. But I look a bit pukey still.

Did you know that my exams are in two weeks? I feel sick at the thought. Believe you me, my fears aren't unfounded either. This course is a <u>lot</u> harder than Leaving Cert., but I've dossed. I'm half expecting to fail Economics and Management too 'cos I really haven't done a tap. I can just imagine all the tongue-waggers and cut-throats 'There's yer wan now: yeah, failed, yeah, and she such a swot'!

Our formal classes finished a week ago but I've continued to go up and down (not on my knees, dum-dum) to WRTC. I've never enjoyed a week as much. I go to the library all day to swot. Most of the class have gone home – Portlaoise, Wexford, Limerick, Kerry, etc., but Killian, Martin, Nuala, Niamh and Dave have stayed. We take breaks from quarter to eleven 'til half past, from half twelve 'til half one, from quarter to three to quarter past three . . . So you see I'm not getting much done but the crack is fab. Killian and myself keep a continual banter going. Last week, we were all in the canteen (on one of our numerous breaks) when a guy from my bus from Clonmel passed. Since Nuala is from Clonmel I asked her out of curiosity who he was. MOOSE, they call him. Now I'll never live it down. Everyone asks me how Moose is. Niamh rags Killian that he's outdone and he replies, 'Yeah, by a MOOSE!'

Anyway, to get back to the exams my timetable is as follows:

Mon 28 May: 9.30 a.m. – 12.30 p.m. Accounts
Tues 29 May: 9.30 a.m. – 12.30 p.m. Law
Wed 30 May: 9.30 a.m. – 12:30 p.m. Statistics
Thurs 31 May: 9.30 a.m. – 12.30 p.m. Management
Fri 1 June: 9.30 a.m. – 12.30 p.m. Economics

The total number of candidates sitting in Ireland is 138. Guess what place I'll get if I don't get something done in the next fortnight? Cathy, please pray for me, won't you?

I met Eleanor over the town a while ago. Spent ages talking on the street. Pick and Bulldog passed. Eleanor looks great and has passed all of her nursing exams. She was telling me about the incident in her room. Did she tell you? Well, if she didn't, I will. Apparently, the police wanted to use her bedroom for surveillance as joyriders were nicking cars in the area. Now, the Reverend Mother thought it would be immoral if Eleanor were to stay in the bedroom with all those young virile males. So Eleanor was banished to the dungeons (oops, I'm getting carried away) – downstairs. But before she went she was careful to remove several unmentionable undergarments (?) from the radiators. Later on, she went back to the room with some other girls to talk to the gardaí. When she opened the door she realised that she hadn't removed everything from the radiators. One had remained behind a chair, which the guards had pulled out. The others burst out laughing and Eleanor turned bright red.

Cathy Cummins' exams are coming up too and she's just as worried as I am. We had a great chat the other morning. She was recalling in sixth class how Tony used to jump over the playground wall for Muriel and we'd all see the bushes shake and Muriel would duck behind the trees, etc.! Doesn't it seem like another age, another time? God, I sometimes feel I was never a child. I always seemed to be so damn sensible. By the way, Catherine thought she saw your sister, Celia, around at Easter, home from London.

Met Margaret Lonergan in the cemetery yesterday. She was there with her da who was painting a kerb. I was there with my maw who was stepping on 'em! Anyway, she said that Greenhill hasn't changed much. She's not doing maths this year at all but lucky for her she's been promised a place in the College of Art again. Meanwhile, B— is housekeeping for the Longs from eight in the morning 'til eight at night for £20, a six-day week. She's absolutely furious but her mother is keeping her to it. At Easter the Grill in Tramore asked her to go down but her mother didn't tell B— at all. I'm sure B— blew a fuse when she found out. (I'm going for my tea now, be back after.)

Hello again. I've finished my tea, watched *Fraggle Rock* and now the news is on. Maw is giving out about politicians. Nothing strange at 63. That's if you don't count Maw and Paw that is. They papered the upstairs room last week. I've sent you a piece of the wallpaper. Gives the dustmen a break! Yesterday, they cut up the kitchen unit (no, not for firewood!). Actually, they were narrowing it as the kitchen is so small. Paw had measured it up and marked it out and Maw came along and scrubbed it off as she thought it was dirt. We went for a walk after that!

Mimi, the cat, is fine even though Paw calls her Mini! We've set grass in the back this year but it's very reluctant to come up. Mimi hasn't helped. For some inexplicable reason she has taken to relieving herself down the back and scrapes clay and grass seed from all angles to hide the evidence, while Maw and Paw do a war-dance in the kitchen, beating on the window. Meanwhile, Mimi doesn't turn a hair though she does wag a tail.

We've gotten very friendly with the new neighbours. Nygel and

Maggie are very nice. I got a lift home from them one evening. The youngest baby is gorgeous. He is really cuddly 'cos he's so chubby. He's called Trevor.

Now for a bit of news. The Clancys and Tommy Makem were on the *Late Late* a fortnight ago. It was fabulous. They had all come together again for the first time in years. They spoke about Carrick too. As you can see from the *Opinion*, they're making a film in Carrick at the moment.

Meanwhile the country is going bonkers over Ronnie Reagan's visit to Ballyporeen in three weeks. I guess there's so much frustration in this country at the moment, what with the recession, unemployment, etc., that auld Ronnie is gonna be the object against which they'll vent their anger. Some people in Galway have sighted missiles being fired off the coast. Maybe Sister Thérèse is right – the Russians are comin'!

Remember Mary F with the long hair? Well, she went out to Boston as au-pair. However, I heard she came home again this week as she hated it out there!

Remember Carmel who was in our French class? Her father died suddenly last week leaving <u>fourteen</u> kids and another on the way in July. To crown it all, his wife went to tell her mother about it and the poor woman got a stroke and died as well. Two funerals in one week is no fun, huh!

Guess what. I finally got a letter from my penpal when I was thinking I'd never hear from her again. She did get married. Somehow, though, I think she's finding married life very different. She says she misses her family terribly.

Now about telly: you'll never guess what they're repeating – *Rich Man, Poor Man*. I'll be glued to it for the next few weeks, exams or no exams! Remember Billy and Wesley and Rudy? Ooooh!

You said you got your goggles changed. I'll have to do the same. I can't see anything now, really. I may be going deaf too! Last Friday morning, I was standing at the bus stop in Carrick on my ownio waiting for the bus. Anyway, a car came along and out jumped this absolutely gorgeous guy – blond, blue-eyed. The car drove off and he turned towards me and smiled and said, 'Hi.' He then asked me something, but I was too stunned to comprehend so I said, 'Sorry?' and he asked me if the bus was coming. Then he asked me was I in the college and again I said, 'Sorry?' He must have thought I was stone deaf. Then he asked me had I gone down the previous day – sports day. He repeated it three times! Gawd, I felt idiotic. He offered me a fag, then asked me for a match and since I hadn't any he had to put his fags away! He told me he was 'in construction'. Sounds impressive, huh? Anyway, the bus came and I never saw him again. Oh, for what might have been . . . if I could bloody well hear him!

New goggles or no new goggles, you probably have eyestrain again after this scrawl. Maw and Paw send you best wishes.

By the way, do you have to stay 'til Sept? How about me and you wandering around Europe? I'll rob a bank and then we can formulate plans. Now, study, here I come – ooh, I feel sick.

Best wishes, God bless,
Lots of love, Mary

PS Sorry about the auld paper but sure I'm a poor auld student, amn't I?

PPS Have you heard anything about Anne's boyfriend, Teddy Bear?

Trégunc

Monday, 21 May 1984

Dear Mary,

How dare you! How could you possibly! I've never in the whole of my life met anybody so nasty and mean and cruel and horrible. Imagine ending a letter with 'Have you heard anything about Anne's boyfriend Teddy Bear?' You must have really flipped your lid to do such a terrible thing! I'll have probably died of curiosity before anybody else writes to furnish some more details. And it's all your fault, so I hope that you're feeling suitably guilty.

In revenge, before the customary inquiries pertaining to your health and that of all the clan, I'm going to be very selfish and pass on my main item of news to you first. There I was yesterday afternoon peacefully knitting (a cardigan for Thomas's birthday in the middle of June), with one eye on *Starsky & Hutch*, when Vivianne asks me if I'd mind bringing a baby for a walk, as her parents hadn't finished their meal and she was getting restless. So off I goes with Jessica in her pram and Thomas hanging onto the side of it, and me feeling like a married woman and singing 'My Bonnie Lies Over the Ocean' and Brahms' cradle song and so on. She didn't seem to object to the English, not to mention my non-existent voice, but then I suppose one doesn't notice such things at three months.

So, anyway, when I came back after an hour or so, Viv had a quick whisper in me little ear. It turns out that the family live in the highest skiing station in Europe. She has a sportswear shop while he's a skiing instructor/guide. And they need an au-pair from October 'til April. Nothing is certain yet but it's most likely that after I finish up here in September I'll take a month's holidays at home and then – watch out ski slopes, here I come!

They seem really nice. There's just the baby and another three-year-old in the family. So if I go I'll learn how to ski and might get to visit Austria and Switzerland and Italy, as the station isn't too far away from all these countries. It's in the Alps.

When the woman goes back to Savoie, she's going to send me some photos and so on. But I don't really know if I will accept. I mean, here in Brittany, I'm far away from everybody; if I go to the Alps, well, that's almost twice as far away, isn't it? Then there's the problem of clothes. Imagine the rig-out I'll need to live there. She was telling Vivianne that during a <u>sale</u> anoraks cost NINETY pounds! And the special boots cost even more. And I haven't a clue yet what amount they'll be giving me.

But I think life'll be more interesting there than it is here. At the moment, as it's out of season, there are only forty people living in the station. But during the season, the 6,000 beds are all occupied. So as you can see it's really big. And people from all over the world go there.

And I really haven't a clue what I'll do about a job after September. I mean, I'm not qualified for anything, and even though I'm good at most things, I'm not great at anything. I was hoping to stay around Carrick, as I miss all of you terribly, but from all accounts, I haven't a hope in hell of getting a job there. And my other choice being London doesn't exactly make the heart beat any faster.

So, I think it'll be six months in the mountains for me,

which should improve, if only slightly, my knowledge of French not to mention life! Anyway, I'll be sure to keep you up-to-date on all relevant information.

And now the formalities! Apologies for the scantiness and tardiness of the last epistle! Hope that this one will make up for it.

For God's sake, do yourself a favour and go and get your lugs tested. I can tell you, if a guy of the description given was anywhere within a ten-metre radius of me, I'd hear him THINKING, not to mention talking. And then, ya silly twit, ya gets on a blinking bus and lets a specimen like that just walk out of your life (okay, okay, so it was you who drove out of his, but the end is the same, isn't it?).

As I hate duplicating what I write, if you want to know about the Romeo of my dreams – literally – or my attempts at mastering the art (?) of donkey-riding, you'll have to phone Sue.

I think it goes without saying that I wish you the very best of luck in your exams. They really sound tough, and even though at times I'm just going out of my skull with boredom and mental and physical inactivity, well, I don't think I'd like to be in your shoes at the moment. Did I mention that I've given up my correspondence course?

You were saying there that the day you wrote your letter the weather was lovely and sunny. Well, even if it was gorgeous here for most if not all of April, it sure as hell is making up for it now. I don't think that the month of May has given us even one really good day. I got a great tan, but am sure it'll be all gone before I can get a chance to put my swimsuit on again, that's if I'll manage to wriggle into it!

You know, I always feel homesick. It's a sorta feeling that's always there, like a bad tooth, and sometimes you get a bit of food, or a prong of a fork (?!) or a sweet stuck in it and wow! It gives you hell! The things that irritate my particular malady include letters from home, or when I see on the *Carrick Opinion* that the Sean Kelly film will soon be shown, or that Gaybo had the Clancy Bros on, or Catherine Cummins reminisces on the Good Old Days.

Or the night of the Eurovision. That was worst of all. I could almost hear everybody in Glen cheering for Ireland, and Nanny cursing (yes!) when somebody gave us a bad vote and saying that it was because of politics, and <u>what were</u> the English crowd wearing and . . . Well, I suppose you know what I mean? And on the Monday morning I remembered the way we used to be – when we weren't gawking into biology books, that is – discussing it all and Margaret Cooney'd be <u>sure</u> to put down the songs everybody else liked.

While over here I was all by myself (like Eartha Kitt) because François and Vivianne were working and the kids were in bed, except for Chrystelle, who was snoozing on the couch and didn't bother anyway to answer my comments.

You're lucky that you get the chance to see people every day. I'm afraid that I've forgotten how to talk and hold a conversation. Now I understand the mentality behind the punishing of prisoners by putting them in solitary confinement. Remember what an awful chatterbox I was? Remember the day Sister Bernadette (ole cow!) chucked me out of her music class because I was blabbing to Annette

Cleary? Enuf sentimentality for now, otherwise I'll start bawling me peepers out and that'll make the ink run!

Shall I make you jealous? No, it's not intentional. I've been on a spending spree lately. I got a gorgeous white jumper with bat-wing sleeves, which is perfectly see-thru and goes with all (?) of my clothes especially my red trousers which I love. (You know I was very hurt when Maeve Binchy* said that my writing was breathless, but I think she was right!) Then the other day, while window-shopping at the Marché (i.e. a weekly event in Concarneau when about fifty stalls are set up in the square), I ended up with white sandals and a matching bag. And y'know those long belts that go around your waist twice and sorta hang loosely, well, I got one of them to go with the black top and skirt that I made. But now I've put the brakes on, which'll be most necessary if I've to get a whole rig-out for the mountains.

Have you been in the 'Uptown' recently? What've they got in the line of clothes? Remember the gorgeous stuff they had in Pat Hickey's as well? Wasn't it there you got your lovely yellow dress?

Thank God I'm not anywhere near B—'s house now. I imagine there's sparks flying in all directions. I'd say B— was/is in a right old humour. I wouldn't fancy being in her shoes. I don't mean to be bitchy, but she did have her head in the clouds waiting for somebody to appear on the doorstep and beg her to go working for them for high wages, etc.

* While at school Catherine had entered a competition and won a place in a writing class with Maeve Binchy.

...eepers out and that...
Shall I make you jealous?
...en on a spending spree. I
...jumper with bat-wings
...u and goes with all(?) of m...
...rousers which I love. (Y
Maene Birely said that
...think she was right!). I
...ou-shopping at the Ma...
...carneum which about fi...
square), I ended up wi...
and y'know those lo...
...waist twice and sort...
...f then to go with the
...ade. But now I've put t
...neccessary if I've to
...ntains.
    Have you been in the
...got in the line of clothes
...had in fat plukey? as...
...your lovely yellow dress
...God I'm not...

I'll ask you in advance to excuse any irregularities which may appear from here on as it's gone 11 p.m. now and my brain is sorta foggy. I've just finished off a letter to Eleanor, which I started a month ago, and while I'm in the humour, I thought I'd add a bit more on to this one. Seriously tho', I'm getting kinda worried about myself. There was a time (when I was young!) when I could hardly wait to get a letter from somebody before replying to it. Now, I don't know, it's becoming more and more like a chore. I hope that this is only a phase I'm going thru and that it will soon pass, as all phases do and must.

And, you know, I really felt like crying when I heard RTÉ were repeating *Rich Man, Poor Man*. When I think of Peter Strauss and all those other gorgeous guys, not to mention, as you did yourself, Muriel Butler. If I remember correctly, she was crazy about Billy while the rest of the class were nuts about Wesley. They had *Scruples* on here on Saturdays at 1.30 p.m. I was delighted and, what's more, saw the first two episodes in their entirety. But the third week, I went to Alain's house to give him his English grind. Vivianne promised to record the last episode for me. Only Chrystelle, who was supposed to arrive from school at 1 p.m., failed to do so, so Vivianne started giving birth to kittens and due to labour pains forgot about her promise. I was absolutely furious. If you can remember how it finished please let me know, won't you, Molly dear? My hand has just about gone to sleep and the rest of me is following suit so I'll shut up now. Sweet dreams – and until tomorrow.

Here I am again! And what a miserable, horrible night it is. What rain for the end of May.

English lessons are going great with Anne. She's a nice kid, but naturally it's easy to say that when I only see her for an hour every week, I suppose.

I may have told you that the first week Marie-Claude suggested (or rather her mother did) that we go out together some time. Well, much as I thought, nothing has come of it. I'm not surprised, really, as I saw her in the distance on the beach one day with a guy, and they appear very friendly. I never did like gooseberries. Just the same, every week we chat for five–ten minutes and even if the conversation is strictly impersonal, well, I've gotten to know her a little bit better. I can see that despite her outward appearance, well, she is rather shy and insecure herself.

As you said yourself, the last time I wrote I was rather down in the dumps. Hope this humour didn't rub off on you. My moods seem to change from one minute to the next. Most of the time I seem to be in a bad humour lately, but then just for a little nothing at all, I cheer up again. Like today when Yvan remarked how bizarre it was that I was cold. Generally everybody else has typewriter teeth while I'm toasting. But the fact that somebody, anybody, noticed I was there and alive and breathing and freezing, well, it made my day! How thick!

I am making a very conscious serious effort to come out of the cocoon I've spun around myself during these past nine months. It's quite hard, you know, trying to take part in conversations with a very limited vocab, but I'm trying and appear to be succeeding. Hell, I'm not going to continue this paragraph any more. It's too difficult to explain my feelings, and in trying to do so, I'm only boring you and wasting paper!

You were saying that you'd phoned Sue. Were you talking for long? I'd a letter from her a week before yours arrived. That's why you'll have to ring her up to find out about the donkeys, circus, etc. When she wrote, I got a few quick notes from two of the girls sharing her house. I suppose you've already heard about all of her new friends. She does tend to go on about them a bit. God only knows when she last mentioned the people I've already met, but her new friends do sound nice.

Am I being bitchy in the following? Sometimes I think she's trying to make me jealous, the way she goes on about Michael. You know, much to my surprise I've even forgotten what he looks like. The main guy's face before my eyes at the moment is Lambert Wilson. He's a French actor who starred in the last film with what's-her-name, Brooke Shields. In *Sahara* he unfortunately wears a beard, which means that his indescribably beautiful smile gets lost in his beard.

Speaking of which (smiles, that is, not beards), guess what else I forgot: Tom's birthday. It's just three days after mine, and this time last year, I thought 14 April would be a date engraved for ever and ever in my heart. But you know it never crossed my mind 'til Eleanor sorta casually mentioned it in her last letter. I mean, I didn't want to send him a soppy card or a pressie or anything, but I feel sad and old and as if I'm made of stone because I didn't remember him. D'you know what I'm on about? I hope you do. Have you seen or heard of him lately?

And while on this subject – Killian. Do I detect a glimmer in your eye that says spring is in the air? What's he like? Is he good-looking or just one of those guys whose face you like without knowing why? Does he take a lot of notice of you? Has he got a girlfriend? Please pass on any comments you feel like making about him. I know if I were still pestering your doorbell ten times a week, he'd be one of our main topics of conversation, so if you feel like dedicating half a notepad to him, I'm all eyes. But I know only too well what you mean about guys who are so friendly with everybody. You never know where you are with them, do you? I mean, is he just being his normal outgoing self, or is he really interested in you? It can be quite annoying, can't it?

Like this really gorgeous guy who works in the café/pub/ ice-cream parlour just beside the beach. The first time I picked up enuf confidence to go in there for a Mars Bar (and a double Scotch!) he served me, and he seemed so friendly and gave me a devastating smile. And after that it was a Mars a week, and a heart down in the dumps if he wasn't there, until I heard that he's the same way with everybody, and that his two equally, or almost equally, gorgeous brothers are the same. If I say that it's because of him I can no longer fit into my favourite summer skirt, will you get the wrong message and be disgusted? His mother lives next door to the restaurant. The bar belongs to her. But, y'see, if I ask Viv if her sons live with her, she'll tease me dreadfully and, what's more, is likely to mention it to his mother. I keep my peepers open every time a car passes into their place, but it's always his mother who drives. But there's generally a lot of traffic around midnight. I guess bats aren't so unlucky after all!

And speaking of which, it's now 12.02 a.m. (no, it didn't take me two hours to write two pages, but TV sorta got in the way). So I'll stick me pen back in me pencil case and try and get some sleep. Believe me, I need it. My appearance has gone to the dogs, and that's an insult to the mangiest dog on the Main Street in Carrick. I want to get up early tomorrow and stick me mop in the washing-machine. Viv has promised to see if it's long enuf for French plaits.

So just take care of yourself. Write back as soon as possible, won't you? Y'know yerself how disappointing it is to see the postman just passing by.

Tell your parents I was asking for the two of them. Think your penpal is absolutely crazy – how old is she? Any word from Annette Cleary? Celia was home for Easter and by all accounts had a great holiday. Did I mention that Pop's company has definitely gone down the drain again – for good? That's all the info I know, though, on that subject.

Excuse the awful scrawl. But at least that way it'll take you longer to read the letter.

All my love,
Catherine

PS Any idea of who's coming to Trégunc for the twinning?

PPS Almost forgot (disaster) – <u>best of luck</u> in your exams!

Part 4

Blossoming

Summer 1984

Carrick

Monday, 11 June 1984

(Lying on my bed 6.40 p.m. on a very dull evening –
how's that for scene-setting?)

My dearest Cathy,

From now on I promise (hand over heart and fingers crossed!)
that I'll never ever apologise for taking so long to reply again.
You'll just have to lump it!

Seriously, though, I'm now on holliers and you know how it is –
what with the spins in sports cars (Ferrari, of course!), dancing 'til
three, shopping in Twiba's, eating in gourmet restaurants – I just
didn't get around to it! (Actually, I don't arise 'til din-dins and the
only gourmet eating I've been doing is fish 'n' chips. But sure, wot
the hell?)

I got your letter during the middle of the exams and, boy, was I
delighted. I used to come home on the two o'clock bus as the
exams were from 9.30 to 12.30. The day your letter came, B— had
come in to see me 'cos her mother was bringing in eggs to us so
she said she'd come for the spin. There woz I, reading the bit
where you said you wouldn't like to be near B—'s house, and B—
sitting beside me, asking what you were saying! She had finished
her housekeeping job the day before and, boy, was she glad. She
hated it there, I'd say. So now she's in Tramore working in the Grill.
Her mother called with eggs (again!) last Thursday and when I
asked if she had heard from B— she told me that B— has dyed
her hair PLUM. Her mother has had a double dose of kittens and
canaries. I didn't know what to say to her as she went on about

how B—'s hair was already a lovely colour and how she had ruined it. But I say cheers to B— – nothing like a bit of madness, huh.

Incidentally, B— is totally cheesed off with Mills & Boons. D'ya know, she really woz waiting for a Sir Galahad. But now she says she sees 'sense'. Actually, I think the fact that so many girls around town have been getting married has troubled her. She's wondering what they have that she hasn't. She also said that if she ever has a daughter she's going to ban Mills & Boons! A definite case of hitting the earth with a thud, don't ya think?

On the subject of the exams – ahem! I got through them but in all truthfulness I doubt if I've done very well (if the others' answers are anything to go by). Oh, well, there goes 'No. 1 in Ireland' down the drain! The results will be out on 6 July.

I really enjoyed the exam week, though, as we were all together again as a class (even if it woz only for the duration of the papers!). Now that it's over (college, I mean) I don't know what to think – whether I liked the class or not. Okay – during the year I really enjoyed the company. It made a change to be able to hold an intelligent conversation with somebody (using big words even!) without being classed a swot. I enjoyed Liam's wittiness, Martin's antics, Killian's comments – but in some ways I don't think I really fitted in. I dunno exactly what it is – it's hard to pinpoint – but I have this niggly sort of feeling that you're not one of 'em. You know, sometimes I felt like screaming at lunchtimes when someone discussed the second new car their mother was buying (cash, of course) for the 999th time, or when they discussed holidays in Spain, etc., or they debated the merits of Mercs over Saabs. You'll never know how often I prayed during those moments that I wouldn't scream. Don't get me wrong, though, it wasn't that I was jealous,

have this wriggly sort of [...]
you're not one of 'em. You kn[...]
like screaming at lunchtime [...]
discussed the 2nd new car [...]
[...]ying (cash of course) for the [...]
[...]en they discussed holidays in [...]
[...]hey debated the merits of [...]
You'll never know how ofte[...]
those moments that I woul[...]
[...]et me wrong though, it wa[...]
[...]calous, it woz just that [...]
[...]hy they felt this need [...]
[...]al possessions 95% of the t[...]
somebody from another planet [...]
[...] wot sort of cars (note the [...]
Imagine their faces when [...]
to hell with those who s[...]
classes don't exist any mo[...]
[...]'ve never been to ACA !!!
To summarise the above

it woz just that I couldn't see why they felt this need to discuss material possessions 95 per cent of the time. I felt like somebody from another planet when they asked wot sort of cars (note the plural) we had. Imagine their faces when I replied! And to hell with those who say that social classes don't exist any more. Obviously they've never been to ACA1!

To summarise the above confused wanderings, I liked them very much as people – as human beings – as fellow students. But a lot of the time, I just couldn't identify with their capitalistic points of view. Ya know, beside them I felt like an absolute COMMIE! For people so young, some of them have really entrenched right-wing views. One of the lads referred to the student union on one occasion as 'a crowd of COMMIE bastards'. They absolutely loathed trade unions and you wouldn't want to mention politicians like Tony Gregory in their presence. A month before we broke up, one of the girls was telling us one lunch time about a crowd of itinerant children who'd been on the bus, so the conversation got round to itinerants in general. You should have been there. You wouldn't believe how much they detest them. 'Dirty smelly creatures', she called them. But somehow I felt in a strange way sorry for some of the class. They didn't consciously want to be snobs. It's a real case of one half of the world not knowing, wanting to know, or perhaps being able to understand, how the other half lives. Listen, I'd better shurrup 'cos I really can't express how I feel on paper about the class. It sounds more stilted than I actually feel. It'll have to wait 'til Babby McCann's ice-cream parlour in the autumn!

I'll never forget the last day we broke up, though – a Friday. I was supposed to come home at two o'clock but I stayed on. We all went (by 'all' I mean about sixteen of the class) to Paddy Browne's.

Believe it or not, but it was the first time I held a full conversation with Joe or the other Martin. John got drunk and Nuala was tipsy. I was busy taking down addresses on the back of a Smithwicks label! At around 4.30 p.m., Niamh and I decided to head into town so I shook hands and bade farewell to Killian, Maurice, Liam and the others. We crossed over a field and the stream. And that's the last I saw of them – walking away across the field. I hope I will remember them in years to come. I doubt if some of 'em will remember my name.* I'll be 'the wan with the glasses' or 'Niamh's friend' ('cos really Niamh mixed better than I did!).

When I was going home that evening, Cathy Cummins, her cousin Annette (who's <u>really</u> a lovely girl) and H— D— were on the bus. Yes, that was H— D—'s name u saw. She got 'dismissed' from the hospital 'cos she failed her block exam. She told me that she was called to the matron's office, given her exam results and asked to leave straight away. Seems a bit suspicious to me. Somehow I thought you'd at least get a second chance. I feel really sorry for her now. She came back to Waterford to do the Health Science exams but she had missed two months of the course down below, so I'd say she found the exams stiff. Also, it will be hard to get another nursing job in Ireland after being 'dismissed' from a Dublin hospital. Poor H—, Sister E— stopped her in the street of Carrick and said, 'My goodness, H—, what did you do?' H— said she felt like telling her, 'Sister, I strangled a child,' just to see her reaction. The Goof is writing away as well. Speaking of which, I met her over the town and she said (as only the Goof can!), 'What are you doing?'

* Mary was doing a two-year commencement course but some of the class were only doing the first year. How much a sponsoring firm was prepared to pay for depended on its contract with the trainee.

By the way, I'll be working in the office in a fortnight's time. Wish me luck. I'll need it.

Golly gosh, I feel so proud. I'll be voting for the first time on Thursday – the Euro Elections you know. I feel 'all growed up', I do!

Thanks ever so much for the photos. Thomas is gorgeous. Believe it or not but I imagined him to be just as he is! That says a lot for your ability to put people down on paper! I really loved the piccy of 'La Pointe de Trévignon'. Just the sort of place to take a stroll on a soft warm day with a tall blue-eyed guy in tow, sun dancing in his hair and sparkling eyes, birds singing and your heart going pitter-patter. Ah, shucks, who needs Mills & Boons?

Are you fibbing or are you really hesitating about going to the Alps and skiing? I know many people who'd jump at it (gerrit? Skiing – jump at it). I would love to be able to ski but knowing me I'd probably fall and break my goggles (not to mention both arms and a leg or two).

Last Saturday week, these two people (a fella and his wife whom Maggie and Nygel next door had asked to clean our chimney for us) came along. He climbs up on the roof leaving yer wan below. There he was, getting ready to knock down soot all over the house (we'd removed the flue), until Maw piped up, 'Where's the soot going to go?' (Bright spark, my maw!) 'Oh, yeah,' says yer wan, and put back up the flue, whereupon soot came flying down it into the cooker, out through the doors and all over the house. 'Where were you?' I hear you ask. Well, I locked myself away until the coast woz clear, then came down to find Maw half laughing half crying, covered in soot. No jokin', for the next three hours we were brushing soot off the settee, telly, etc., washing curtains, tablecloth, windows – ourselves. Even the most famous monument since Nelson's Pillar – your coffee-table – was smothered in a blanket of soot. But never fear, it looked as good as new after a belt of a wet rag!

Maw, Paw and Martin went on a trip to Galway yesterday, organised by Brother Agnellus. The bus broke down in Kilsheelan – tee-hee. They all got off and had to wait for an hour for a mechanic. Meanwhile, Biddy Sheehan demolished a packet of bikkies while sitting on a grass verge. She then couldn't get up so Mrs Butler went to help her. The latter sank into three inches of tar while doing so, tried to move but fell in on top of Biddy. Meanwhile, frantic efforts were made to dig the shoes out of the tar. Finally, they were retrieved and Maura Mullins produced a roll of toilet paper with which to wrap them up. Meanwhile Biddy still couldn't get up. <u>Three</u> men attempted to lift her but she fell back, up went her legs in the air and details of her knee-length bloomers were made known to all and sundry. People lay down on the road laughing – the main Clonmel road I might add. Note – this all happened <u>before</u> they reached a pub.

Dav and Teresa next door also went. Anyway, they were all home at 10.45 p.m. having played music (Paw on the box) for busloads of Yanks in Durty Nellie's. Matty won a coffee set in Salthill. Just the thing for your coffee-table, huh?

By the way, the Leaving is going on this week. I sent a card to Tina and notelets to Cooney, Suzanne and Dolly. Boy, I don't envy them, do you? Such an anti-climax.

Gee, weren't you lucky to miss all of the ballyhoo in Ballyporeen? Nancy and Ronnie were over. Martin had to go up with the Civil Defence, but you wouldn't believe the security. Some poor priest was torn out of his house 'cos he dared to open a window at the wrong time. All the houses in Ballyporeen were emptied and searched at ten o'clock. It all passed off peacefully enough. But you'll never guess who said the Mass in Ballyporeen? Father Ryan: we had him in the Presentation NS. I've sent a piccie. I felt really sad as I heard him speak, remembering all the Masses he said for us in the Pres. Remember the way we used to practise in the Assembly Hall and how we'd march up class by class? Now I pass that very same school and feel like Methuselah's cat!

Listen, I'm going to watch *Dynasty* now; I'll see you tomorrow!

Hi again. It's now 2.01 p.m. on Tuesday. I've just been listening to the news. Great excitement in North Waterford/South Kilkenny. Five criminals kidnapped a woman in Dungarvan after ransacking her house and then abandoned her, after kidnapping three others and locking 'em in the boot. They then broke into a shop in Aglish and locked up the owners in a coal shed. Then went on to Mooncoin and did the same thing. And this isn't even *Dynasty*!

Speaking of which, *Dynasty* is gone to the dogs! Blake is in danger of losing Denver Carrington as he can't pay back a loan; Jeff and Fallon are getting remarried; Sammy Jo has come back from New York; Steven is married to Claudia; Kirby (who is going to marry Adam) tried to kill Alexis; the latter was being blackmailed by Mark, who is now dead 'cos last night he fell or was pushed off the balcony of Alexis' flat. Phew!

Guess what, Anne-Marie's got a new fella called Robert. He's from Westport and he looks after thousands of pigs on a pig farm. Maw, Anne-Marie and I were sitting on our garden seat last Friday night when he came along. My first impressions are that he is very nice.

Now, finally, I bet you've been going out of your mind about Anne – well, so have I. I've phoned Sue twice hoping to get some more info, but there was no one there. I met Anne herself one day and was about to ask her about 'Teddy Bear' but two friends of hers came along and so I didn't get a chance. But, gee, you wouldn't know Anne. That day you should have heard her talking to the others about – FELLAS. Imagine, our Annie! All I found out is that she met him in Kildalton and he is from Adare and I'm not sure but I think she went out with him once or twice.

Listen, that's about all for now. I'll write sooner next time, okay? Keep me posted about the skiing, etc. Maw and Paw send you their best.

God bless.
Lots of love always,

Mary

Trégunc

Saturday, 16 June 1984

Mary, chicken,

You can blame your fortune on receiving this letter on my misfortune at having a terrible tummy-ache. Y'see, there's a concert in Concarneau this afternoon, which is given by the music students. And dear Delphine is one of this gifted bunch and has for the past month been practising her piece from 7 a.m. 'til 8 p.m. Vivianne had a beautiful navy smoking made for her. And even me this morning, well, I went to Concarneau and having visited every clothes shop there finally got a print blouse to go with a cream skirt for the big occasion. But due to the torture I'm now undergoing (i.e. sheltered from the TOASTING sunshine by the covered terrace, listening to the radio, forcing down a slice of fruit tart, despite the agony, which is due, I think, to eating too many apples), my ensemble is laid out tidily on my bed, and I won't get a chance to have a last glimpse at Delphine's gorgeous music teacher. Sob, sob, sob.

And while on the subject of the other sex . . . well, where do I start here? With Richard? With Michel? With Anne-Marie's new fella? Yes, with the latter, I think. I'd imagine by the time you get to write back to me (better be soon!) it will have developed a bit more. Don't forget to keep me up-to-date, not to mention filling me in – i.e., what does he look like, how old is he, where does he live, etc. But please pass on all the latest in romance, won't you? If you, like me, haven't any news of your own in that field, then trespass elsewhere!

If you've been in touch with Sue recently and, as I hate repeating what I write, I hope you have, then she may have told you about Richard. In brief detail, he works in the bakery next door, is quite good-looking, and always seemed very nice. But then, well, I hardly ever really spoke to him. Anyway, about three weeks ago, I was going for a walk, and he came along in his car, stopped and said he was going to Ireland for Sept and what was it like, etc. So anyway the conversation ended with his promise to pick me up on the following Saturday night. I'm sure you can imagine how happy and delighted and nervous and so on I felt. My first real date and in France too.

To make a long, boring, depressing story short, we spent from ten 'til two bar-hopping while not <u>one</u> of his friends opened their mouths to me all night, and Richard himself acted as if I wasn't there and went off playing pool. Remember what a bad-tempered cow I am? Well, at 2 a.m. I asked him if he wouldn't mind dropping me off on his way to the next bar. (It was only thirty–forty miles out of his way.) And the . . . – cannot find suitable description of what the French call a 'salaud' – was SURPRISED I wasn't enjoying myself. As you can see, even after three weeks I'm still mad at him. As a matter of fact, I should entirely avoid mentioning this subject as doing so doubles my pulse rate (with <u>anger</u>) and all resulting heat released is not good in such warm weather.

I try to avoid him as much as possible, but as he lives, or rather lodges, ten metres from the restaurant, that can be difficult as you can imagine. The couple of times I have seen him, I just said a quick hello and kept going. But as well as that, you see, I'd borrowed a tape from him, and was faced with the problem of how to give it back, avoiding all conversation in the process.

Please don't think I'm being vain or big-headed, etc. But, y'see, he was very insistent that I go out with him again and, frankly, even if he is really nice when his pals aren't around, I'd rather stay at home and knit! I mean, he was well up on the speech line and all, and said I was 'charmante', 'ravissante', 'terrible' (that's a compliment here by the way!) and that he wasn't able to sleep since I said I'd go out with him, blah, blah, blah. Well, he can take his bloody poetry book, and choke himself on it! And good riddance to bad rubbish! Hey, careful, pulse rate's just tripled.

So, I was most eager to avoid all conversation while giving back his tape. But one day, I noticed he was just about to go somewhere in his car, rushed for the tape and got thru the whole ordeal with polite comments and nothing personal. Phew!

The other day, Thomas and I, making the best of the arrival of a beautiful summer, were heading off for the beach, when who should we meet en-route mais Michel, the guy who works in the kitchen for the summer. So what should be more natural than that the two of us proceed – not hand in hand, but together nevertheless – to the golden seaweedy sands, where we stayed together for two hours 'til he had to leave.

Well, what can I give you in background info? Not much, really. I know he worked in St Phil last summer – he told me he left the day I arrived, which gave us a good laugh. He did his Bac last year, but is repeating again this year. As a matter of fact, he started it Thursday. He's very shy and quiet and I think I'm REALLY going to like him a lot. When the Bac's finished he's going to work in the restaurant for the season.

I've got a (impulsive!) feeling that he's clever and intelligent. But maybe that's only because he looks like – guess who? Gerard. Well, maybe not really like him, but he's got dark curly hair and, Mary, the most beautiful blue, blue, blue eyes. Pity he wears goggles! And his smile is really lovely and makes me feel happy. Do you know what I mean?

I don't know much else about him really, except that he lives near the restaurant and goes to boarding-school in Quimper, and hates apples that are in any way bad, and gets *Reader's Digest* every month – he gave me a loan of one, which I'd already read (Viv gets it too) but I'm just a girl who can't say no!

I went for a spin on the bike (Chrystelle's) last night and he passed me in a car. He was driving and had three or four friends with him. He gave a huge big wave, which, while not making my night, cheered me up.

(Oh, a beautiful thrush is eating some crumbs just a metre from my feet. I love the terrace: it has a beautiful atmosphere and is full of bright flowers and singing birds, and as it's just on the side of the road I can watch the world passing by!)

I wish I could ask Vivianne about him, but she's like your maw, and'll just tease me dreadfully and in front of everybody too and I'll die of embarrassment and'll end up hiding myself in the bathroom 'til 1 Sept. And, anyway, maybe he's just one of those Tom, Michael, Gerard people, y'know, who are so damnably friendly and smiley and nice with everybody. And maybe nothing'll come of it – whatever the 'it' might be. And maybe if something does happen, I'll just be disappointed and cross, the way I was with Richard.

Am I boring you with all this nothingness? I hate the insufficiency of pen and paper! Y'know, I'd swap all the beauty of my present position for a hard chair in the ice-cream parlour with rain pouring down the windows and a real conversation with you (excuse me, I'm going to cry!).

Can I say something without offending you? Remember last year when myself and Sue used to drive yourself and Anne nuts dinner time after dinner time with our endless conversations on Michael, C— and so on? Remember our minute dissections and analyses of <u>all</u> of their actions and words? Even though nothing was ever said out in the open, I got the impression you weren't happy with us. Well, looking back over your letters of the last few months and your comments on Anne in your most recent letter, all I can say is, 'Welcome to the club!'

Isn't it a great, marvellous, uplifting, depressing, agonising, etc., feeling? I think just the mere fact of knowing that they're (boys, dum-dum) there, well, it changes <u>everything</u>, doesn't it? But it can be so frustrating trying to figure out what they're thinking and, more importantly, what they're thinking of you.

Wish you were here! But in the meantime, let's do something this summer that'll take over all of our conversations for Sept. Get the drift.

I never realised that people like your classmates still existed. I thought 'Commie bastards' died in American films during the fifties. I believed all people of our generation wanted a world where everybody is equal and the words 'class distinction' needed to be looked up in dusty dictionaries. Just shows that ivory towers have very thick walls, doesn't it?

But to tell the truth, I understand great riches, i.e. three or four cars per family, regular holidays abroad, and all that type of stuff, the same way I understand the cruelty of the Nazis and Auschwitz during the last war. D'you know what I mean? Perhaps I am narrow-minded but I tend to think that most people's lifestyles are more or less like ours. Sure, there are some who can afford to have beautiful clothes for the summer, etc., but otherwise, with some exceptions, well, we're all the same. Thick, aren't I?

Don't take the next paragraph wrong. I never really put myself out looking for info. on the WRTC but I always felt it was a kind of inferior college, where people (like us!) who couldn't really afford to go to Trinity, etc., went to get the first foot on the ladder. So, I was really amazed when you first started telling me about all of these silver-spoon-fed friends of yours. But I suppose that's life, isn't it? And everything you learn in third level doesn't come out of books.

Had a letter from Celia a fortnight ago. She was working in an office for a couple of weeks for experience. Apparently, there's this guy who worked for the same company and she got sweet on him. But unfortunately she's now back in college for a block period and probably won't get to see him again for ages. She seems to have gotten on really well at work. Everybody bought her a present for her birthday in May, and when she left, they all chipped in and got her some expensive French perfume, and they went out for a drink together. I believe she had a great holiday when she was home at Easter. I felt homesick reading her letter afterwards.

Oh, yes, about Avoriaz – that's the name of the skiing station for the ignorant among you! About a fortnight ago, there was a documentary on TV about it. Wow! It's just gigantic, full of hotels and chalets. All in modern architecture. Really beautiful. I'd understood that the family were supposed to write back to me a few weeks after I'd seen them. But Viv says, no, they're supposed to do so at the end of the summer. That makes things rather difficult for me. I'd prefer to have everything fixed up now. I mean, supposing I'm in Ireland when the letter arrives at St Phil? By the time Viv forwards it, well, that'll be cutting things close for the beginning of October. But anyway, for now, I'm going to enjoy the sun, and let the snow take care of itself.

What else have I in the line of news? Oh, yes, went to Quimper with Viv the other day. While she went to get her hair done, Thomas and I did some window shopping. I felt great. I wore my new(ish) red trousers with my white jumper, which has bat-wing sleeves and is see-thru and I love it. I had a pair of white sandals that I got cheap in Concarneau and a matching white bag. Without boasting, well, I knew I was . . . presentable. I love that feeling, don't you, when you're all dressed up and looking your best and you can feel people's eyes following you? (No smart comments, okay!)

Only when we got back to the car again a tyre was flat. And this dishy hunk came to our rescue. Only the spare was flat too. So Viv disappeared in search of a garage with Thomas, while I was left car-sitting. Two hunks who parked their car in front of ours came up to me with offers of assistance. Unfortunately I had to decline. And they disappeared into the sunset. In the end another Knight in Shining Armour ended up putting on the flat spare and we limped off to a garage.

Even though the day was ruined, well, my faith in men was restored. Did you know that there are still males who, despite the curse of women's lib, come to the aid of Ladies in Distress? I didn't, but now I do, and feel happier because of it. Soppy and thick, aren't I?

Thomas was three on 11 June. Vivianne's grandparents (yes!) are currently staying at her parents' and so were invited for the festivities. François made a beautiful strawberry cake, which went really well with the champagne – Dom Ruinart no less. Only £25 a bottle! The most expensive in the restaurant's cellars. But afterwards there was a minor earthquake or, at any rate, I noticed all of the walls shaking!

A couple of days later

I put this letter aside in the hope that something worthwhile committing to paper might take place over the interval, but nothing did. Except that the weather was absolutely gorgeous and I've been practically living on the beach. Consequently, my tan is coming along nicely.

Please write soon. I'm sure you'll have more time to do so on account of the holidays. Have a great summer, and keep your eyes and ears open for gossip, won't you?

A big hello to your parents.

Lots of love,
Catherine

PS Hey! Almost forgot, your job! Tell me every little thing that happens won't you? And GOOD LUCK!

PPS Were you watching Roland Garros? I only saw a little bit but it was great. Dreadfully disappointed that Connors lost. But looking forward to Wimbledon, are you?

Carrick

Sunday, 1 July 1984

My dearest Cathy,

Here I am again all set to compose another letter – except this time I have very little gossip. You know, I half believe that the entire population of Carrick has decided to watch their Ps & Qs just to deprive you of it. But never fear, I'll rack my brain for sommat.

Meanwhile, the door is open and I can hear the birds twittering, the cars passing to the seaside, children laughing (or crying) and flies buzzing. Martin is in Clonmel at the horse show (Civil Defence duty). Maw is in bed snoozing and Paw woz reading the Sunday paper up to a while ago.

I thought perhaps there might be tennis on the goggle box today but there wasn't. I haven't seen much of Wimbledon so far 'cos of my job (more about that later) and they didn't cover Roland Garros here at all. Ya know, it's so long since I've played tennis that I'd probably hit the racket with the ball!

(Deviation: ya never said what instrument Delphine plays – a tuba?!)

To get on to the subject we all seem to be preoccupied with at the moment (romance – not the weather, dum-dum), I'll start with Anne-Marie's new fella – Robert. Talking to me this morning, she said he's gone home for the weekend. It's a fair journey on our bad roads. To enlighten you a bit more: he's about two inches taller than me, fair hair and nice eyes (as eyes come – usually with pupils, irises and eyelids! Tee-hee. Sounds like a Macra stock-judging competition). Seriously, though, he _is_ quite nice. Just an ordinary everyday sort of guy.

Somehow I think they're all trying to get me fixed up over here. There I woz the week before last, coming home with wallpaper for my room, and coming up the road I could see a gang of the neighbours congregated around our gate ('Where else?' I hear you ask!) while across the road Adam was painting (again!). As soon as I woz in earshot it started, 'Hey, Adam, here she's comin' now'; 'Wouldn't ye make a fine couple – she papering and you painting?' – to which I replied, 'Yeah, how romantic.' Adam's mother was worried in case ADAM would be embarrassed, but nothin' about poor Muggins. To her amazement, he <u>didn't</u> get embarrassed and now she's conjuring up that perhaps he 'has notions' about me. D'ya ever hear the likes?

Meanwhile, Maureen's (from across the road) nephew came home yesterday morning to Maureen's. I dunno if you remember him from other years but he's dark and good-looking (sounds like an ad for Guinness!) and who should be talking to Maureen when he should arrive? Only my maw! I was mortified as I heard her say, 'Come over to my place now. I have a grand daughter for you with a good job an' all.' How in God's name will I be able to face the fella if I meet him?

Now to you, Kitty chicken. You're a crafty one all right; leaving out <u>all</u> the details of the return journey home with Richard. Come on, I want all the sordid details of your goings-on (if it wouldn't be detrimental to my innocence, that is!). Do you really expect me to believe he kept his hands on the steering wheel (especially since he called you 'ravissante')? Wait'll I see your grandmother and she'll have you home and in a convent before you could say, 'Je n'avais fait rien.' If Reggie could have seen ya . . .

Now, Michel, he seems a <u>nice</u>, <u>respectable</u>, <u>sensible</u> boy. Seriously, though, Richard doesn't sound much different from your typical Irish Romeo (or Irish Paddy or Tom or Dick). Are you sure 'terrible' is a compliment?! Anyway, keep me up-to-date on any further developments. After all, someone has to look after yer welfare! Meanwhile, happy hunting (in its truly literal sense!). Something tells me you're onto something good – I can feel it in me bones (if I could only find my bones).

I nearly forgot about the Macra Field Evening. It was on last Thursday week (21 June). I wasn't intending to go but there I was getting ready for Mass that morning (for Corpus Christi) when Sue's letter came. Briefly, it said, 'Ya better be at the Field Evening tonight or else!' At Mass, I met Anne Cummins (who incidentally had the most magnificent outfit on – from Moons of Galway, no less). She woz going too, so I said, 'Ah, here, what the heck?' Sue called that evening and her father drove us down to the mart. We were greeted most heartily – by a powerful stench of cow dung! We walked around and then Eleanor came along. We walked around some more, did a few quizzes and competitions. I helped Mary Rose with the 'Guess the Peas' competition – I carried the money – what else would an aspiring accountant do? Tom said hello (incidentally, he's suffering badly from shingles at the moment). It was peculiar to see all the old faces again – you know, sort of like walking backwards through time. John was trying to persuade Eleanor to milk an artificial cow by saying that the present leader was a girl. Eleanor said, 'Sure that must be me?' and he replied, 'Ah, no, this wan was good-looking!' Eleanor was bucking!

Sue, Eleanor and I then snook in for tea and after that we sat into Eleanor's brother's car. We had a good natter there. Seems Sue had some trouble with her college landlord over the state of the house. I guess she'll tell you all about it, though, herself.

Anyway, we then went on to Piltown to a dance. Gina, Dale Haze and the Champions were there. You know, this was my first proper dance – all the others were improper! There we met Anne Maher, Mary and Helen, too. I saw Alma Grace, talking to Teresa Dungan, and saw Tricia(s) O'Shea and Colleton. Had a good time dancing around. Got a few slow dances from Willy Parle (a friend of Martin's!). Then this guy asked me out. Now, it's a policy of mine never to refuse a fella a dance unless he's drunk or has been put up to it by his mocking mates. So I sez to meself, 'Here goes.' Oh, Kitty chicken, he held me so close I could barely breathe and he insisted on dancing cheek to cheek. It wouldn't have been so bad only for he mustn't have shaved for a few days and his chin was like sandpaper! Ugh! He started to talk then – well, shout, actually, as we were near the stage. Turns out he was from Mullinavat. He asked me wot I was doing so I told him and he said, 'Yeah, begorrah, ya look fierce brainy!' No kidding. The song ended but I couldn't get away as:

(1) We were in the middle of a packed floor.
(2) All the surrounding couples were giving each other mouth-to-mouth resuscitation – must have been the heat!
(3) He had a vice-grip hold of me.

After the second song (which seemed to go on for ever), I broke away (perhaps I dug him in the ribs – I can't remember).

'Ah, come on,' says he, 'just the next wan.'

'Ah, no,' says I.

'Pleeeze,' says he.

'Naw,' says I.

'How about seeing me later?' says he.

'No thanks,' says I.

'Another night maybe?' says he.

'No,' says I, 'thanks for the dance, though,' and with a toss of my head I glided across the floor and walked out of his life for ever!

I really enjoyed the night, but I don't think I will join up the Macra full-time again. It still amazes me that such good-looking fellas have no other interests. Pity (comments, please).

You know you said I might have been mad with you and Sue last year. Well, it wasn't that way at all if I recollect rightly. In some cases, perhaps some of the fellas mentioned just didn't interest me. And in retrospect, I woz probably envious in relation to some others! (By the way, I know <u>exactly</u> how you feel when you speak of the frustration in determining wot certain males are thinking.)

I finally got my head examined – well, eyes, actually – in Waterford. I'm waiting to hear from the medical card crowd at the moment but the optician seems to think that contact lenses are very suitable for me so I have to wait and see. Incidentally, Maw asked me what the optician looked like but I couldn't see him!

I'm going for my tea now (ta-ra).

Meant to ask you – how often d'ya get letters? The poor postman must have his shoes worn out or have you hired out your own postbox?!

Did you know that Gemma (Anne-Marie's sister-in-law) has a new baby girl? Everyone's delighted especially since she lost Sandra. The baby's getting christened today. Do you remember Jim from the bakery at the top of Bridge Street? He's very bad at the moment – suspected cancer of the throat. You know, a man called Micksy Whelan from Seskin died a while ago and everyone thought it was my paw!

I think you're right about WRTC. Most of the courses down there are looked down upon by the unis, etc., but our course is different because it is a <u>professional</u> course not taken by the unis anyway. So that's why my classmates are a little different from other WRTC students (except for the computer students).

Well, that's about all except to say that I've been working in Gilligan and Co for the past week. I was nervous as hell going in on Monday at nine thirty. Couldn't see anyone around so there I was with one leg in the front hall and the other in the office when Jim Gilligan walks into the office through another door. We wag paws and he says, 'I'll bring you upstairs now.'

'Ho, ho,' sez I. 'I knew it!' I followed him up the gold-coloured carpeted stairs, I look into his eyes, he smiles, he opens the door, we walk in and there before us – <u>a big wooden desk</u>. Actually, Siobhán Babington was there too. There are four desks in my office: one for me, one for Siobhán, one for Anne Connolly and one for Greta from Galway. (They all are in their twenties, except Greta who is forty-ish.) In walks John Walsh and starts me working on cheque journals.

Basically, I have to make records of all cheques paid, analyse them, lodgements made, analyse them. Downstairs work Angela Danagher and Margaret Friend. Margaret phoned me up to ask me whether I'd like tea or coffee! Next door to our office works Martin O'Sullivan. Upstairs works a guy whose name I can't remember but I think he's Michael and is very nice. Out the back office works Jim Raleigh from Dublin. Up the stairs is the computer room. And that's about it. I also work on milk accounts, doing analysis of Avonmore statements, etc., and goods accounts, recording purchases of goods from Avonmore. Greta is really patient and shows me what to do.

The atmosphere is really nice over there and I think I'll like it as the others are very friendly. The guys are very mannerly – holding doors, etc. Pity they're married! I got my cheque from John on Friday – IR£40. Not bad really for the amount of work I do. I was using an adding machine all week, which uses tons of paper in printouts, and I finally found out on Friday I needn't use the paper! The only problem is that I think most of their clients are farmers and if so my training will be deficient in other areas, i.e. industry, sole traders, bank audits, etc., but I guess I'll wait and see.

I'm glad I'm returning to the college this autumn but I suppose it won't be the same without certain people. I'm toying with the idea of writing to 'em but I think I'll wait until after the results – when I'll have an excuse. Well, that's about it for now. <u>Missing you a lot!</u> I'm going to take September off when you come home, by the way, so take care until then.

Lots of love,
Mary

PS Martin came home from the horse show. Brenda Hyland, the Rose of Tralee, got kicked by an ass, broke her nose and sprained her wrist up there. Civil Defence brought her to be bandaged and get her nose splinted and guess what – she's in a beauty contest tonight!!

Trégunc

Friday, 6 July 1984

Dear Mary,

I was delighted to get your letter today. I've been expecting
one for the past week and had me poor peepers worn out
watching for the postman. I was really disappointed when I'd
nothing at all day after day. In fact, I was beginning to give
up hope of ever again hearing a word from you. But then I
kept saying to myself, 'Give the kid a chance, she's probably
up to her eyes in work.'

Where do I start? With my news or with yours? Well, first,
I should congratulate you on your job. It sounds great. Be
sure and keep me up-to-date on it, won't you? I never realised
it was so big there and that they had so many people working
for them. But do you like it yourself? Is the work interesting
and do you get to apply what you learnt in college? Do tell
all.

I'd imagine you'll be surprised at the manner in which this
letter arrives. Hopefully Lena delivers it by hand! I'd love to
see your face. Anyway, it turns out that Lena is doing au-pair
for a family about a mile down the road. Only she has an
interview for nursing in Dublin the third week in July.
Unfortunately, she couldn't change it, so she's to go home for
it. So I'm going to give her this letter and also one for Sue.
Can you be an angel and phone Sue for me?

I am just DELIGHTED that Lena is here. She's terribly nice.
I never dreamt that I'd actually get to know her one day, but
we go to the beach together every day and it's just terrific

having someone of my (or, indeed, ANY) age with whom I can talk about everything and anything. I don't think you can have any idea of how terribly lonely I've been since I left Ireland and how much I missed you and all the girls. And I just feel so happy again being able to say what I want to and talking about fellas and period leaks and clothes and, and, and . . . do you know what I mean?

Anyway . . . remember anytime we ever saw her in Carrick, we always whispered, 'That's Lena!' in bated breath, as if she were some kind of Sophia Loren or Brigitte Bardot or whomever. You know the way she always looked so sophisticated and sure of herself and kind of . . . above us? Well, she's not a <u>bit</u> like that. She's as nervous and self-conscious and shy as the rest of us. Really, it's true!

She said that for the first fortnight or so when she arrived, she was so lonely she bawled her eyes out every night. Then one day at the beach, these guys were playing football, and the ball hit her. They came over to apologise and she kinda got to know them that way. Otherwise she said she'd have never 'got in' with anybody by herself.

So this year, naturally enuf, she wanted to look up her friends again, but it took her <u>three</u> days to pick up the courage to go over to the beach where they were. So, off we went to see them yesterday. I mean, they are so nice and friendly and welcoming, not to mention gorgeous and tanned. Just sensational. I've already given Sue a run-down of them, so I'd imagine she'll read the letter under your roof and'll probably give you a synopsis or if I've said nothing nasty about 63, the letter itself!

But there's this guy called Hervé and, in Lena's words, I fancy him. Lena with her big mouth went and told the people she's staying with that I was 'in love' with him. It's funny, but I don't consider I've ever been in love. I've always called it 'having a crush', even when it was quite serious like Tom and Michael.

Anyway to get back to Hervé, I don't know – it's just a feeling that, well . . . How do I explain it? I like him a lot. I don't know him but I like him. I noticed him looking over at me a few times and we chatted about books for a few minutes. I'm really keeping my fingers crossed that it'll get off the ground. I really want it to.

I was talking to Lena about him afterwards. She said she doesn't know him very well either, as she only saw him a couple of times last year. Unlike me, she thinks he's gorgeous-looking. I think he's just attractive. But she offered to find out from his brother Olivier if I have a chance. I offered to rub sand onto her sunburned shoulders!

Well, that was yesterday. But, you know, I think Thierry is also worth a mention. I don't fancy him. But I think he's terribly nice. He's the best-looking of them all. Raphael is next. He looks like a guy out of the *Blue Lagoon* type films – you know, you'd sink the ship yourself to get stranded with him. He is just marvellous with kids. I said that to Lena and Big-mouth went and told him. Luckily enuf, I hadn't added on that I think he'd make a terrific father. Lena said that he's terribly possessive when you're going with him – you know, clinging onto you and all that. It was very obvious that he's presently going with one of the girls in the gang.

him. But I think he's ...
hon el, Raphael is next.
the Blue Lagoon type films.
yourself to get stranded w...
with kids. I said that to ...
told him. Luckily enough,
he'd make a terrific fat...
bly possessive when you're g...
of you and all that. It ...
sently going wild one of t...
They seem totally unreal...
think that the Irish te...
typical contact, unless yo...
me body. Over here, it's no...
rest of all, all the gu...
heek when they met (Be...
ups shake hands. And I ...
anybody's roaring sewm-su...
and

They seem totally uninhibited over here about . . . well, bodies. I think that the Irish tend to be rather shy about physical contact, unless you're actually going out with somebody. Over here, it's not a bit like that. I mean, first of all, all the guys kiss all the girls on the cheek when they meet (beautiful custom!) and the guys shake hands. And there's no awkwardness when everybody's wearing swim-suits or anything. It's just all natural and ordinary and not a bit dirty.

Well, where was I? Oh, yes, that was yesterday. So today we went over to 'their' beach to see if they were there, but most of them, including Hervé (sob, sob), weren't. You see, a lot of them have gone to the South of France on holidays. Lucky things. So, they'll be away for the next two weeks or so!

By the way, Thierry is supposed to be going home with Lena. If he does BE SURE AND GET A GAWK at him. It's worth it. I've warned her not to let him out of her sight in Carrick. I also suggested she bring a dark-haired baby with her. Give the town something to yap about for the summer.

If (and I'm keeping my fingers and toes crossed) anything interesting happens with Hervé, I'll be sure and let you know, okay?

Unlike the LeClercqs, the family Lena is staying with have piles of friends, one of whom is seven months pregnant and swims and sunbathes topless! Incredible, huh?

There's these people from Kilsheelan I met on the beach on Monday. Matter of fact they came over on the same boat as Lena. Anyway, they are just really nice. Most days, I spend about an hour gossiping with them. I get to catch up on a bit of the local news. I didn't know them before, but I do now. They've got three kids who are lovely. We got around to talking about food today and, y'know, afterwards I think I'd have sold my soul (if I have one!) for a big plate of spuds, cabbage and bacon, followed by a whole pot of tea and five or six slices of Nanny's apple tart! Isn't it true about not appreciating things until you no longer have them? Y'know – 'Gratitude is flowers on a grave.'

Lena says I now talk English with a French accent. I feel totally demoralised because I talk French with an Irish accent! D'you think I'll have to give up talking altogether? I think that'd be harder than giving up eating! Bruno keeps slagging me, because every time he sees me I'm eating. I really must do something serious about it.

Am I beginning to annoy you with 'Lena this' and 'Lena that'? If so, apologies. Hopefully the next time I write Hervé'll take precedence over Lena!

I must say (old chap) the Macra thing sounded like a real reunion of the class of '83. Did you all get misty-eyed with reminiscing or was it looking ahead to the future? Off with the old and on with the new kinda thing?

(You know the pregnant one I was on about? Well, she was wearing a T-shirt/dress with the Pink Panther on it and 'Tout le monde est fou pour mon corps!' Funny, huh?!)

By this stage, the only way my poor peepers will stay open is if:

(1) I stick matchsticks in 'em.
(2) Hervé puts in an appearance.

And as both of these are as unlikely as me growing wings and flying to the moon, I'll have to shut up, but before I go, I picked up the mail on the way to the beach and consequently read your letter there. I started giggling like hell when I was reading your conversation with yer man at the Macra thing. Audine and Chantal (pregnant) who were lying next to me must have thought I was a right nut. Mind you, they just might have put it down to the fact that I was Irish!

See you tomorrow, I suppose! Nighty night, sleep tight. And please, God, don't let the mosquitoes bite!

Sunday, 8 July

Hi again! I just have twenty minutes or so to get down a few happenings before I go and break my neck in a donkey derby.

Well, as you most likely know, the crowd from Carrick are over this week for the town-twinning celebrations. So last night there was a 'Fest Noz' (céilí) for them, and naturally enuf myself and Lena went. It was held just down the road from me in a big barn, commonly used for such happenings. The two of us walked together and just as we got to the place this crowd of girls were coming towards us. One of them threw herself at Lena, so that was when I copped on they were from Carrick.

How do I describe what I thought of them? My God, they were all babies when I left home, clad in orange and brown uniforms. And there they were last night with punk (almost) hairstyles and Bananarama-type clothes. We did a thing that would never have occurred had we all met at home: we gathered around in a circle and blabbered away like a pile of long-lost friends. Who was there? Jean Crowley, Denise O'Sullivan, Miriam Walsh, Carole Reddy, nobody that I really knew. Oh, yeah, Claire Fitzgerald. All girls anyway; mostly third and fifth years.

Anyway, they didn't know I was from Carrick. They thought I was French! I ask you! Everybody said I spoke English with an accent. But I find that rather incredible, don't you? But then somebody copped on that I was from the tuck-shop back in school and that cleared matters up a bit. Incredibly, I've been told my tan is rather noticeable.

So this was around 10 p.m. And we all stood around in the field where the barn/shed is situated, yapping away. There was a French girl there that I know so I was talking to her for ages as well. Miriam Walsh is staying with her.

Lena knew quite a few of the French guys, so our conversations kept getting interrupted by them – no complaints. By eleven thirty, we were fed up of it there, and decided to go to the pub about a mile up the road to see if any of Lena's friends with cars were there. We wanted to go to the Quartz, a nightclub, but by the time we got to the Suroît all of her gang were gone. So we just had a coffee and went back to the Fest Noz.

I think I have to go now. But maybe I'll have time to tell you of the utter misery and torture one of the girls (who will remain nameless) inflicted on me last night. I pity you living in the same town as her! She never stopped whining about the family she was staying with because she wasn't allowed to stay out 'til 4 a.m. The whole way to the Suroît she kept on and on about all the guys she'd pinched from her friends. And how much she drinks and smokes and how often she goes out per week and all the boyfriends. God, I wish I'd pushed her into the bloody sea. With specimens like her, I'm not in the least bit surprised that most girls (or at least the decent ones!) won't admit they're from Carrick. If the people here could have understood her, I'd really have felt ashamed. I <u>really</u> feel sorry for the two chaperones in the group!

Anyway, we got back to the Fest Noz at about 12.30 a.m. There we once again met three guys Lena knows. They're really nice. So we stayed talking to them 'til two. It was all very friendly and chummy and funny. I really enjoyed myself. We were sitting on the grass and the moon was shining and the atmosphere was just terrific. Unfortunately, Hervé wasn't there, sob, sob. Hadn't expected him to be.

But you know what really struck me? Everybody (except the three above mentioned) of around our age was just blind drunk. I was really disgusted. Nothing but young fellas swaying and staggering around the place. I suppose, though, that it is pitiable. Gilles said it was because there's nothing else to do here. But, Mary, it was just incredible. I mean, how could you live like that, never remembering if Saturday night existed or not? I think the drinking problem here as concerns young people is much worse than at home. But then I suppose I didn't really see a lot of what went on after closing time in pubs at home. They close here at about 1 a.m. and the niteclubs do so at 4 a.m.

I was saying to Lena how awful it was and she said the crowd she hangs around with never get to that stage. Thank God, otherwise I doubt I'd enjoy myself all that much here. See you later if I'm still alive!

Hi again, I'm terribly sorry for taking so long getting back to you. I'll cut out all the useless chatter and just give you the news. Donkey derby consisted of three rounds – fell off halfway thru the second. My only distinctions being that I was the only foreigner to ride AND I was the first to fall off. Met most of the Carrick crowd again. Actually, I've bumped into most of them two or three times since Saturday night.

Last night was great. At about 10 p.m., myself and Lena got all dolled up and went off to the Suroît. I borrowed these gorgeous trousers from her as well as a beautiful V-necked jumper. She did my make-up and I really felt confident. Great way to start the evening. Anyway, when we went into the pub, the two Nolans were there. So we went and sat with them – real case of the Irish sticking together. They're very nice. Next thing is Laurent, a guy Lena vaguely knew last year and whom we met last Saturday night, came in with a friend. Laurent has long blond hair, but he is something else, beautiful mouth, lovely blue eyes, great taste in clothes. So he came over and said hello and started talking to us. Great flirting going on. At first I vaguely suspected that he was after me, but then it hit me that it was Lena he wanted. Please don't think this upset me. I think he's fantastic, but I've no feelings in the romantic line for him.

So about one o'clock the two of us got up to go, and when we kissed goodbye, Laurent hung onto me and asked me if I'd help him to get thru to Lena. Now you know me, I'd do anything to help true love. So guess the result, I ended up walking home with Patrice, his friend, while the other two walked off in front. Patrice is terribly nice. I think he wanted to 'get off' with me but, well, I didn't feel that way about him, so it was no-go there. Just before we got to Lena's place, there's a wall. So, the four of us ended up yapping on that 'til two. The guys then walked me home again, and guess what we did en-route – visited the graveyard. Crazy, huh? But I'm beginning – for the first time – to feel really happy here. At last I'm beginning to meet people of my age, and I'm beginning to feel like a human person again. Great feeling.

I MUST tell you about the people Lena's staying with. They're just out of this world. He's called Alain and is shoving on for forty, I think. But you'd give him at least ten years less. I don't know when I last saw somebody so gorgeous-looking. Hopefully, I'll be able to lay my paws on some photos for the end of the summer. He's a bank manager. She's thirty-five-ish – really friendly and cheerful. Great dress sense. Works in a sailing school. Ronan is a beautiful kid. Just a year older than Thomas. Tends to be bold at times, but I like him just the same. I'm practically living in their place at the moment. The house is fantastic.

Alain is on the twinning committee. But he says nobody knew I was here. In fact, nobody can believe I've been here for ten months without meeting anybody. The Le Suavés said if they'd known I was here they'd have asked me to go out with them and all that. Lena gets on great with them. She's already been out to a family dinner, and she only here a week!

The two of us went to Concarneau yesterday afternoon. She ended up buying a beautiful ensemble of skimpy top and beautiful gathered trousers. They're white background with cream and black tiny motifs. She looks great in it.

I got a beautiful outfit of a top and trousers. It's pink material with barely noticeable big white flowers. It really suits me. I thought I'd look like a pregnant elephant in it, but I don't. I hope to be going somewhere for 14 July so that I can wear it.

Change the subject a bit. Did you get to see much of Wimbledon? I didn't even see one match. I mean, the weather was beautiful here the week it was on so I was at the beach the whole time (my swimming is coming on great). And I really wanted to watch the finals but, on account of that blasted derby, I couldn't. Just as well anyway, if Connors was beaten so humiliatingly! Had a letter from Celia today. She went to the courts one day and saw a lot of the big names playing. Lucky thing. Unfortunately for the past three days the weather has been just awful. All the water is going to get cold again and it just after heating up and all!

Lena is just about to go so I'll have to finish off. Please write soon, forgive the scribble, take care of yourself, and get on fine with your job.

Lots of love,
Catherine

Late July 1984

Though Catherine received a letter from Mary, sadly it later went astray.

Trégunc

Friday, 3 August 1984

Dear Mary,

Where do I start? A thank you for your letter or a telling off for its tardiness? God, I thought you'd never write and I've so much to tell you.

Firstly, and most importantly, last Saturday, for the very first time in my life, I fell in love. It's like nothing – absolutely nothing – I've ever experienced before. Sure, I know I've had crushes, one of a three-year duration, but I mean, they are incomparable with what I feel for Mike.

If you've ever really fallen for a guy, you'll be able to understand my sentiments, but then can one ever really understand how one feels at such a time. I mean, everybody from Shakespeare to John Lennon have tried to do so. And they haven't really come up with any explanations, solutions or antidotes, so I doubt if I will either.

I know next to nothing about him. He's called Mike – Michael – and is nineteen–twenty-ish. He doesn't resemble Robert Redford but he has got something so attractively beautiful – even now I don't have to close my eyes to see him, and his smile. But I've fallen for him VERY, VERY, VERY heavily. And the thing is, he's terribly shy and . . . hell, why aren't you here so that you can see everything for yourself, and save me these difficult explanations and so that I can cry on your shoulder?

Right, start at the beginning. He came to the beach a couple of days with the rest of the gang, but apart from the parable with what I feel for

If you've ever really fallen for
my sentiments, but then can
one feels at such a time. S
b John Lennon have tried to
up with any explanations, solut
S will either.

S know next to nothing about him.
9-20 ish. He doesn't resemble R.
ng so attractively beautiful.
eyes to see him, and his
VERY, VERY heavily. And the
... hell, why aren't you here s
for yourself, and save me
that S can cry on your sh
Right, start at the beginni
couple of days with the r
m the usual greeting, we
Then on Saturday, there we
......d out on our bowels

usual greeting, we didn't have much contact. Then on Saturday, there were almost ten of us all stretched out on our towels, and Mike was just across from me. And I suddenly looked at him and said to Lena, 'Hasn't he got beautiful eyes?' And then I just fell in love. Simple as that.

That night twelve of us went to a nightclub in Quimper. It was really great. I freaked out like I've never done before. Myself and Lena made sure the rest of them kept on their feet.

Anyway, at about 2 a.m. the 'slows' came on and I kept praying that HE'D ask me out, only time was passing and no sign of him doing so. So Lena goes and has a little chat with Raphael, and comes back with the info that Mike is interested in me, only he's really shy in front of his friends. Lena said I should ask him to dance. But, well, I couldn't ask a fella to dance. Only time was slipping away, and I was getting desperate so I whispered in his ear, 'I've never danced a slow in France, can you ask me?' So he did, and an hour later when the second set of slows came on, he pulled me onto the floor (the dance floor!) and the rest made up the most beautiful night of my life! I'll go into more detail when I see you in Sept.

We came back with Thierry and the fecking eejit dropped me off first outside the restaurant with the words 'Home, sweet home.' Talk about a thinkless, stupid, senseless idiot!

Went to the beach on Sunday, and when he came, he put his towel right beside my one – and fell asleep! Could have killed him. Later this other member of the crowd, Gilbert – who's an immature, rough, annoying pain in the neck – came along and started pestering me. Afterwards Marie-Thérèse – a really nice girl – said Mike looked absolutely furious.

But the problem is he's unbelievably shy, and doesn't say or do anything when the rest of the gang are there. At least, everybody keeps telling me he's shy. And I hope they're right, and that he reacts the way he does because of that and not because he's not interested.

Anyway, at about six we went to the Suroît for a coffee, and to make plans for going out that night. Mike seemed very concerned that somebody would call for me. You see he lives about twenty km away himself. (Did I mention he's in the army, and was only down home for a few days?)

So, I was picked up around nine, and we went to a pub in the town where they all live, i.e. Riec-sur-Belon. Mike acted as if I didn't exist. The same thing happened when we met up with the rest of the gang in another café/pub. At about eleven thirty he just said goodbye, he was going home to bed, and walked off.

When Olivier and Marie-Thérèse dropped me back home I walked up to the beach by myself and bawled my eyes out 'til one in the morning. I'm just so crazy about him and felt so hurt by his indifference, especially after the night before.

Sylvia and Lena say it's just because he's afraid to show his emotions in front of the others. Also he had to go back to the army in Lille – nine hrs by train – on the Monday, so he was 'pissed off'. PLEASE excuse the expression. It's a quote and I can't find a better explanation except maybe – oh, God, I hope so – he'd 'found' me and had to leave so soon. I believe he'll be here on holiday for the last two weeks in August. I really hope so, and that if he is, things will go okay between us. Be an angel and keep your fingers crossed for me, won't you? But I'd better warn you, even though I'm looking forward so much to seeing you all, I'm liable to bawl my eyes out over him for the first week when I'll be home.

In an effort to console myself over his absence, Lena and I went to a nightclub with a few others. It wasn't great – too small and poky. Too many people, not enough space. Just the same I got into the humour and probably lost a few kilos dancing. Got to bed at about five and had to get up again at eight thirty. I'm wrecked since. Could've killed the DJ! We asked him twice to play 'High On Emotion'; he promised us he would and didn't. Went up to him afterwards and said very politely, 'Merci pour avoir joué le disc.' He just smiled! Pig!

Thursday, 9 August

Excuse the shaky hand. Just had a row with Chrystelle and still suffering from reaction and temper. It'll take me five minutes or so to cool off.

You know, the day Lena walked into the restaurant I was, well, I don't know exactly what word to use – worried, I suppose. They'd said so many things about her that I was sure she'd turn out to be a right cow. You should see them now – fawning all over her – and guess what, asking her to replace me in September. Talk about a laugh. But she knows as well as I do how fickle and what absolute brats they can be.

Every day Lena comes up here or I go down there and often the both. If Marie-Pierre or Alain, her bosses, are there, they chat to me and treat us like adults and tell us to make ourselves at home, and do we want a cup of tea and so on.

One night, Alain even went and made it for us. But when she comes in here, Viv hardly says hello to her. It's terribly embarrassing for the two of us, as you can imagine. I'll go into more detail when I get home. It takes too long to explain on paper.

The other night (Monday) I finally got to see the inside of the area's snobbiest, classiest, chicest nightclub, the Shogun. The whole thing was a wash-out for me for many reasons; one of them being I'd just caught the flu. Anyway, next morning I was informed that my dear papa had phoned. They had told him I'd gone out, just for that night, for fear of him being one of those strict types. Ironical, huh? Anyway, he'd said he'd phone back on the Tuesday. So, 10 p.m – I drag me weary limbs off my sick-bed to hear his distant voice. Guess where he was? A few miles outside Paris! (Gasp!) That's what I said too! Apparently he's set up yet another company with another guy – something to do with cleaning ceilings – and they were over here on a job 'til today. He wanted me to try and get over to see him. Unfortunately due to my illness (serious!), financial state (critical!) and the train journey length (six hours each way) I'd to refrain. Work out too much just for the one day even though he is worth it.

Sunday, 12 August 1984 (on enclosed postcard)

Dear Mary,
I started a beautiful letter to you ten days ago. In it I told you all about Mike, the first guy I've ever fallen in love with. Only it didn't work out, and my heart is in smithereens.

What's more, Vivianne is 'out' with me and I don't really know why.

As a result, I'm sitting here all by myself in Concarneau feeling like the loneliest person in the world and trying to hold back the tears. And such a short while ago, I was walking on the moon.

I miss you all terribly and am looking forward to seeing everybody in a couple of weeks.

If a miracle happens and I recover my morale, I'll finish my letter and send it on. But don't hold your breath and don't believe 'It's better to have loved and lost, than never have loved at all.' It's not true.

Yours miserably but in the anticipation of seeing you real soon,

All my love,
Catherine

PS Say hello to your folks for me.

COULEURS DE BRETAGNE
Coucher de soleil à Argenton
Argenton at sunset
Argenton beim Sonnenuntergang

Dear Mary,

I started a beautiful letter to you 10 days ago. In it I told you all about Mike, the first guy I've ever fallen in love with. Only it didn't work out, and my heart is in smithereens.

What's more, Vivianne is "out" with me and I don't really know why.

As a result, I'm sitting here all by myself in Concarneau feeling like the lonliest person in the world and trying to hold back the tears. And such a short while ago, I was walking on the moon.

Trégunc

Thursday, 23 August 1984

Dear Mary & Sue,

Just a quick note conveying my apologies and explanations to you both. I'll be polite (as usual) and start with the apologies. Firstly, for this letter meanly addressed to the both of you, but lately I find that time is worth all the timepieces in the world in gold. Hence, I find myself unable to send you both separate accounts of the more or less same thing.

Secondly, the postcards you probably received last week. The day I wrote them was most likely the most miserable day I've ever survived, without exaggeration. It was a beautiful sunny Sunday, and all the birds were chirping away like hell . . . But the night before, I'd copped on that Mike, a guy I was VERY serious about, and who gave the impression of feeling the same way about me, was only amusing himself with me, on a weekend off from his military service. So my heart was in smithereens over that, and I only glued the pieces back together a couple of days ago. The thing is, they're not firm yet, and if I see him again, the whole thing is liable to fall apart. So, I'm keeping my fingers crossed 'til the end of the month!

And on that self-same Sunday morning Vivianne said to me that she didn't want to see me the whole day. I could do what I liked, just get out of the house. That was (or so she said) because I'd woken her up when I came in at 4.30 a.m. Talk about an overreaction! Personally I think she was just taking all of her problems out on me.

So, that left me (broken-hearted and all) with a day off on a Sunday, with nowhere to go and nothing to do and in a half mind to pack my bags and come home. And, what was worse, Lena had gone away for the day with the family she's staying with so I couldn't even cry on her shoulder!

In the end, I thumbed into Concarneau, did a bit of flag-hopping, bought a few post-cards and sat down at a terrace café to write them home to you. Hope there weren't any crumbs or tea-stains on them!

I was thumbing for at least twenty minutes on the way home, when this <u>beautiful</u> black Talbot Matra came and passed me out! Next thing is, the very same car approaches again, stops and in I climb. Should have seen the driver – out of this world! Young and handsome and charming and intelligent. Anyway, he dropped me off at the front door. That brightened my day up considerably. I mean, I was in need of being brightened up.

The third apology is to Sue, for the fact that I'm sending this to Number 63, and to Mary, who'll have to spend 10p on a telephone call, unless it just happens you've already made plans to see each other.

Anyway, apart from all of this gibberish misery, what have I in the way of news? Oh, yes! Played in a football match, where us girls were dressed as boys even to the point of moustaches, and the guys turned up in skirts and make-up. We won the first match against the crowd in dustbin bags, but the lads from the kitchen flattened us in the second round, and they went on to win the final. Great day, but very tiring, and painful. And that night we went to a nightclub.

So, for three days afterwards, it was sheer agony placing one foot in front of the other.

Had a vinegar shampoo one night in the Suroît. They all thought it most amusing, esp. Thierry, who did the pouring. Had my revenge the next day, though, on the beach. François very kindly permitted me to help myself to a raw double-yolked egg . . .

Also Lena's boyfriend's friend (if ya follow!) was here for a few days from Paris. I have NEVER seen anybody so good-looking, so nice, so funny, so talented, so intelligent. I mean, he's just incredible. The French invented a phrase especially for him – 'super-chouette, super-sympa'! Unfortunately, he's gone back home. But his family have got a fortified castle in the centre of France so IF things work out we'll spend a weekend there. And what's really great is that Eric does winter sports every year and this year there's a good chance he'll be going to Val Thorens where I'll be au-pairing. By the way, don't read any romantic implications into this because there aren't any, even if he did give me the crêpe flower out of his ice cream the night we went eating pizzas!

On Monday, I'll have been here for exactly a year. My God, the summer passed so quickly, and looking back on it now, the winter did too. But it didn't seem like it at the time! I'm hopefully doing something to celebrate.

A fortnight ago, one of the lads celebrated his nineteenth birthday (actually that was the first night I met Eric, when we went to the pizza place). Afterwards, we went back to his place, and opened a bottle of champagne at two in the morning. The only thing that ruined it was that I was still nuts about Mike, who was sitting just a few places down from me, so I felt rather . . . Choose a suitable word yourselves!

Lena got both her Leaving and a place in a nursing school. Delighted for her. (How did Michael do?) Marie-Pierre and Alain gave a dinner for her last Sunday. Jean-Christophe was invited as her partner – naturally enuf. Mine was Loïc, a gorgeous doctor (GP) from Concarneau. Had a great afternoon but ate too much – so did everybody else. Marie-Pierre's cooking is fabulous.

Am I boring you with all this nonsensical meaningless jabbering? Please reserve places for me in both the ice-cream parlour and the Central Grill and our usual haunts for the second week in September.

Excuse the fact that I haven't answered any points raised in your letters. Not intentional I assure you both. But, anyway, I'll have all of September and two weeks in October to do so.

All my love to you both, and to your families. See you in a fortnight or so!

Tons and tons and tons of love
Cat
Kate
Catherine
Pink Panther

These are the names I usually answer to over here.

Epilogue

Summer 2015

Mary

Catherine came home on 1 September 1984. We had a precious few weeks together, the highlight of which was hitching a lift to Limerick in a chicken truck to see our beloved Chris de Burgh in his Man on the Line concert. Then she headed back to France, this time to the Alps. Though we didn't know it in 1984, Catherine would never return to live in Ireland.

I progressed with accountancy, qualifying at twenty-one. I toyed with the idea of moving to London but I didn't want to be too far away from my ageing parents. As luck would have it, as I approached my mid-twenties the International Financial Services Centre was taking off and many of the large accountancy firms were hiring. So, in 1990 I moved to Dublin to work for Arthur Andersen. I went on to work in aircraft leasing with the Irish subsidiary of a Japanese firm, Nissho Iwai. This led to my current role (head of finance) at the Irish Stock Exchange – ironic, considering my worries of turning into a capitalist thirty years ago!

Being a hopeless romantic meant I never gave up on my search for Prince Charming, which led me to kiss some frogs during my twenties and into my thirties. At eighteen I was sure I would be a spinster if I had not walked up the aisle by twenty-four. Along the way I came to realise that I was complete and whole as a woman in my own right. Nonetheless, as I approached my forties, I found my soul-mate – a funny, handsome Dubliner called Charlie. I don't have children of my own but Charlie has two daughters and three sons (and two grandsons to date), whom I love dearly. That her true love would turn out to be a separated father of five was definitely not something eighteen-year-old Mary could have got her head around!

The letters between Catherine and me have opened a window to my eighteen-year-old self that I have found incredibly moving. There's something about approaching fifty and losing your mother that makes you take stock. Reading the letters has made me do that on the double: I can see how much I have changed and how much I have stayed the same. Thirty years of experience has given me a broader perspective and I am more open-minded than I was in 1983. I am also less insecure, having a clearer view of who I am and what I stand for. I have learnt to accept myself, warts and all. I'd like to think my values have remained the same. The more I learn the more I realise I don't know.

Our eighteen-year-old selves would have thought our almost-fifty-year-old selves completely over the hill. Back then, I thought of life in terms of a destination: heading towards that age of perfect maturity. Now I know it's all about the journey. Approaching fifty, I'm still on my journey and will be to the day I close my eyes.

The changes in Ireland in the intervening years have been immense. The internet has revolutionised so many aspects of our daily lives – communication, travel, shopping and music. Cheaper flights have made the global village a reality. Social and legal change has also been huge. And yet emigration has come back again to haunt us. Like myself, Ireland is on a journey and has a way to go.

The letters have brought back wonderful memories of love and laughter shared with friends and family, many of whom are no longer with us. Back then, we thought they would be around for ever.

Mostly the letters remind me of the true value of friendship and how it can last a lifetime. Catherine and I have stayed close. These days we rarely write long letters. Instead we stay in touch by phone and social media.

In 1974, Catherine was a 'bossy big-sister' type. These days she's no longer bossy but I still regard her as my big sister, even if she is only six months older! The next fifty years will be great fun and I hope I get to spend at least some of them in Catherine's company.

I hope you enjoyed meeting our eighteen-year-old selves. I hope that you have a best friend too.

Love,
Mary x

Catherine

I never meant to be a permanent emigrant – travelling and living abroad was something I was going to do for a couple of years before settling down. I believed that I would return to Carrick-on-Suir, marry and have delightful children, who would wear the same school colours I had hated through my teen years – brown and peach.

And a big part of that vision of my future back in Carrick was Mary. I imagined we would continue our Saturday dates, perhaps replacing our youthful ice-cream treats with trendy cocktails as we matured into our twenties and thirties.

But the road I followed took me further and further from Carrick. While au-pairing in the Alps after I left Brittany, I met a French family who had emigrated to Squaw Valley, California. They were looking for an au-pair for their two children, and as I still didn't know who I wanted to be when I grew up, I saw this as an opportunity for more travel. Six months quickly turned into two years, during which I spoke more French than English. In due course the children outgrew the need for full-time care, but I remained in the Sierras. By now, I had fallen in love with skiing and the outdoor lifestyle. For the next fifteen years, I worked in the hotel industry and met people from all over the world.

As the letters show, I was an even bigger romantic than

Mary (she agrees!). Though my youthful passions were intense, luckily they were not lasting. As I reread letter 27, all about the lost love of my life, Mike, the one who broke my heart into 'smithereens', I was amused to find that I could not remember a single thing about him, or about our short-lived romance. The eighteen-year-old me believed that if I had not found 'the one' by my mid-twenties, I was doomed. As I approached my mid-thirties, after many romantic heartbreaks and disappointments, I gave up on love. But, like the cliché, when you stop looking, your prince will find you. Mine was a divorced father of two teenaged boys who showed up on an all-ladies snowshoe outing, innocently invited along by a mutual friend. In August 2004 I walked up the aisle as a harpist played 'When Irish Eyes Are Smiling'. It was a small wedding – I didn't invite anybody from 'home' because I didn't want to be a bride and California tour guide in the same week! Sadly, Mary's mother Peggy had had a brain haemorrhage that April and was still very ill, so Mary couldn't be there.

The following year, after too many years of dealing with the reality of life in the ski industry – high property prices, uncertain employment, shovelling snow – Rod and I moved to Bend, Oregon, in the Pacific Northwest. I became a first-time home owner and now work in food services in our local hospital.

As a girl, one of my favourite television shows was *The Oregon Trail*, a story about the early settlers in the western United States. The ford on the Deschutes river was originally named Farewell Bend by those using the wagon trains – they waved goodbye to each other at the curve in the river as some followed it north and others headed west – and that gives Bend its name. It seems an appropriate home for a wanderer.

Mary and I were both well into our forties, and watching the sun set into the Pacific Ocean, when my dream of us sipping trendy cocktails as we put the world to rights came true. In spring 2009 Mary and Charlie made a trip to the west coast and Rod and I drove down from Oregon (450 miles) and met them in San Francisco. She had visited me in California twenty years earlier, in the fall of 1988, not long after she finished her final accountancy exams – her first major overseas trip. We toured around northern California and went on a camping trip to Yosemite. I have awful claustrophobia and cannot sleep in a tent. So, I would have my body inside the tent, with the zipper closed firmly to my neck and my head outside. There are a lot of bears in Yosemite, not to mention the deranged killers of our overactive imaginations. Poor Mary lived in constant fear of waking up to a headless tent-mate each morning. Despite my best efforts during that trip, I couldn't get her to relocate to the States!

I had paid one sad visit to Carrick in 1991 – when my father died, too young, of cancer. I would not visit Ireland again until 2006 when Mary's parents, Peggy and Mickey, welcomed Rod and me into their home. Peggy served tea and apple tart and said 'tis' a lot and Mickey played the button accordion. Except for the shiny new sparkler on my left hand, it was as if I had never left. Like so many Americans, Rod is part Irish – a Shanahan on his mother's side – so we celebrate St Patrick's Day every year, and as we do, Rod and I still talk about that day in Peggy's kitchen as one of our best memories of Ireland.

I am looking forward to the next half-century and the future adventures. I am over thirty years and six thousand miles from the life and letters Mary and I shared. But when we talk on the phone it's as if the years and miles don't exist . . . and we still keep an ear out for 'yer wan' listening in!

Catherine x